THE DOLCE DIET

LIVING LEAN COOKBOOK
VOL. 2

by MIKE DOLCE
with Brandy Roon

conradjamesbooks.com

Printed in the United States of America.
ISBN 978-0-9849631-9-5

Edited by **Brandy Roon & Sarah Veit**
Cover Design by **Zack Sherman**
Interior Design by **Brady Scott**
Professional consultant: **Samantha Coogan, MS, RDN, LD**

NOTE

TABLE OF CONTENTS

BREAKFAST

LUNCH

ADDITIONAL DRESSINGS

DINNER

SIDES & SNACKS

SMOOTHIES

DESSERTS & BAKING

THE DOLCE DIET

VOL. 2

by MIKE DOLCE
with Brandy Roon

Introduction

In your hands you possess all the tools necessary to fulfill your dreams. There is no greater force on Earth than the power of nutrition. Many of life's ills and ailments can be reversed and even prevented through quality meal planning.

Over the next few weeks, as you settle into THE DOLCE LIFESTYLE, you will see a dramatic change. You will notice energy where you once felt fatigue. You will notice bright eyes where you once had dark circles. You will notice shapely, strong muscles where you once had soft and saggy skin.

I truly believe proper nutrition is the key to all things in life. In fact, I have devoted my life to seeking the best possible nutrients and finding unique and creative ways to make them dance together in a flavorful tango that tastes almost too good to be healthy. But it's not!

You may know many of the world's greatest athletes utilize a variety of these same recipes to prepare for professional and Olympic competition, but the science supporting these meals can and should be enjoyed by all!

Mothers and fathers, weekend warriors and grade-school glee club members can all experience the same life changing nutritional advantages that world-class athletes do simply by eating some of the most delicious recipes you have ever tasted.

Please, take your time to experience each meal. Feel free to improvise with these recipes to make each suit the exact needs of yourself and your family. Food is meant to be fun, and it is meant to be shared with those you love.

I could not be more proud to spend a few minutes with you in your kitchen each day, knowing that we are feeding your family the healthiest foods on the planet – a move that will set them up for true success in all facets of life.

From my family to yours with love!

-Mike Dolce

BREAKFAST

NUTRITION PER SERVING | **Fats: 20g • Carbohydrates: 53g • Fiber: 10g**
Protein: 13g

Almond Butter & Fruit Pita
Serves 1

Ingredients
1/2 banana, sliced
1/4 cup fresh strawberries, sliced
2 pieces of your favorite whole wheat or gluten-free pita bread
2 Tbsp. almond butter

Directions
Split pita bread open and toast.
Smear almond butter inside and pack with banana and strawberry slices.

Note: Apple slices also taste great!

NUTRITION
PER SERVING | Fats: 31g • Carbohydrates: 40g • Fiber: 6g
Protein: 27g

Bacon & Egg Breakfast Grilled Cheese
Serves 2

Ingredients
2 eggs
3 Tbsp. almond milk (or milk of your choice)
dash of Pink Himalayan sea salt
dash of cracked black pepper
3 tsp. grass-fed butter
4 slices whole wheat or gluten-free bread
2 slices organic American or sharp cheddar cheese
4 slices turkey bacon, cooked

Directions
Whisk together eggs, almond milk, salt and pepper in bowl. In medium pan over low-medium heat, add in 1 Tbsp. grass-fed butter then egg mixture and stir until set. Divide eggs, bacon and cheese over two bread slices and place remaining bread on top to form sandwiches. Put separate pan on low-medium heat. Add 1 Tbsp. butter and place sandwiches in pan. Toast each side and heat until cheese is melted.

Bacon & Egg Spread With Toast
Serves 2-4

Ingredients
6 hard-boiled eggs, peeled
1/4 cup mustard
2 Tbsp. green onion, finely chopped
1/4 tsp. Pink Himalayan sea salt
1/4 tsp. fresh cracked pepper
2 slices turkey bacon, cooked and crumbled (optional)
4-6 slices whole wheat or gluten-free bread, toasted

Directions
Place eggs, mustard, green onion, salt and pepper in large bowl and mash with fork. Once creamy, put into serving bowl and sprinkle with bacon. Serve on toast.

NUTRITION PER SERVING | Fats: 18g • Carbohydrates: 43g • Fiber: 5g
Protein: 11g

Banana Flaxseed Pitbull Pancakes
Serves 4-6

Ingredients
1 cup Pamela's Baking & Pancake Mix (or similar brown rice mix)
1 large egg or egg alternative*
3/4 cup water
1 Tbsp. coconut oil
2 bananas, chopped (add to batter before pouring into pan)
1/2 cup ground flaxseed (add to batter before pouring into pan)
dash of cinnamon

Directions
Follow the pancake directions on the back of the mix.
Use coconut oil for the mix and to cook the pancakes.
Serve with Fresh Berry Syrup.

Add more water to batter for thinner pancakes. Less water for thicker pancakes.

*EASY EGG ALTERNATIVE (This egg substitution is equal to 1 egg.)

1 Tbsp. ground flax seeds
3 Tbsp. water
Stir together until thick and gelatinous.

Fats: 2g • Carbohydrates: 2g • Fiber: 2g •Protein: 2g

NUTRITION PER SERVING | **Fats: 22g • Carbohydrates: 64g • Fiber: 9g** **Protein: 8g**

Blueberry Coconut Buckwheat Bowl
Serves 1

Ingredients

1/4 cup organic buckwheat
1/3 cup unsweetened shredded coconut (keep a palmful of coconut on the side for toasting)
1 cup water
1/4 cup plain almond milk
sprinkle of Saigon cinnamon
1/3 cup blueberries (fresh or frozen)
1 Tbsp. agave or honey

In a small pot, bring water to a boil and add buckwheat and coconut. Reduce heat and simmer.
After about 3 minutes, when buckwheat starts to thicken, add in blueberries, mix and cover. Mixture should thicken in about 4-5 minutes. Remove from heat, stir and cover.
In a small pan, toast the extra coconut flakes and set aside.
Back to the buckwheat: Drizzle in agave, cinnamon and almond milk (be careful not to make the mixture too thin). Buckwheat tends to keep thickening even after removed from heat.
Put in bowl and top with toasted coconut flakes. Enjoy!

NUTRITION
PER SERVING | Fats: 10g • Carbohydrates: 34g • Fiber: 5g
Protein: 5g

Blueberry Pitbull Pancakes
Serves 4-6

Ingredients

1 cup Pamela's Baking & Pancake Mix (or similar brown rice mix)
1 large egg or egg alternative*
3/4 cup water
1 Tbsp. coconut oil
1 1/2 cups fresh blueberries (mix into batter before pouring into pan)
Follow the pancake directions on the back of the mix.
Use coconut oil for the mix and to cook the pancakes.
Serve with Fresh Berry Syrup.

Note: Add more water to batter for thinner pancakes. Less water for thicker pancakes.

*EASY EGG ALTERNATIVE (This egg substitution is equal to 1 egg.)
1 Tbsp. ground flax seeds
3 Tbsp. water
Stir together until thick and gelatinous.

FOOD | FACTOIDS

COCONUT OIL

Coconut oil contains lauric acid. The only other source of lauric acid is in human breast milk. Lauric acid is a medium chain triglyceride that is better absorbed in the body compared to other saturated fats, and can help lower cholesterol. Coconut oil also acts as a great anti-nausea remedy.

NUTRITION **PER SERVING** | Fat: 15g • Carbohydrates: 86g • Fiber: 15g
Protein: 13g

Breakfast Bowl

Serves 1

Ingredients
1/4 cup oat bran (or buckwheat)
1/4 cup blueberries
1/2 cup strawberries
1/4 cup raisins
1/2 sliced banana
1 Tbsp. all-natural peanut butter or almond butter
2 Tbsp chia seeds
2 Tbsp hemp seeds
1 pinch cinnamon
1 cup water

Directions
In a medium saucepan, bring 1 cup water to boil.
Reduce flame and mix in berries, oat bran and seeds, stirring often until desired consistency is reached.
Mix in raisins and cinnamon.
Pour into bowl and add peanut butter or almond butter and top with banana.
Add in a dash of almond milk or water to thin out oat bran if desired.

NUTRITION PER SERVING | Fats: 10g • Carbohydrates: 58g • Fiber: 8g
Protein: 7g

Cashew & Quinoa Berry Bowl
Serves 2-3

Ingredients
3/4 cup dry quinoa
1 pint organic strawberries, sliced
16 oz. fresh organic blueberries
1/2 cup cashews, chopped

Dressing
2 Tbsp. honey or agave
1 tsp. balsamic vinegar
1 Tbsp. fresh lime juice
dash of Pink Himalayan sea salt

Directions
Cook quinoa according to package directions.
Place fruit and cashews in a large bowl.
Mix the dressing ingredients (honey, balsamic, lime juice, salt) in a small bowl.

Add quinoa to fruit and mix in dressing. Divide amongst serving bowls and enjoy!

NUTRITION PER SERVING | **Fats: 26g • Carbohydrates: 64g • Fiber: 9g Protein: 5g**

Coconut Fruit Cups
Serves 2

Ingredients
1 mango, chopped
1 peach, chopped
2 kiwis, peeled & chopped
1/2 lb. grapes
1/4 cup pecans, crushed
1/2 cup grated unsweetened coconut

1/4 cup fresh squeezed orange juice

Directions
Combine ingredients and mix well.
Put into small serving bowls.
Refrigerate for 1 hour.
Serve.

BREAKFAST

NUTRITION
PER SERVING

Fats: 23g • Carbohydrates: 43g • Fiber: 8g
Protein: 16g

East Coast Breakfast Toast
Serves 1

Ingredients
1 egg (or egg alternative)
1/4 cup almond milk
2 slices bread
coconut oil (as needed)
dash of cinnamon

Directions
Coat pan with coconut oil and place over low heat.
In bowl, beat eggs and milk together with fork.
Dip bread slices into egg mixture and soak through.
Put bread slices in pan and heat until lightly browned.
Be sure to flip them over to cook both sides.
Repeat until all bread slices have been browned.
Top each bread slice with cinnamon and fresh fruit, or serve with Fresh Berry Syrup.

Note: If cooking for more than one person, simply double the recipe as you see fit.

NUTRITION
PER SERVING

Fats: 27g • Carbohydrates: 58g • Fiber: 3g
Protein: 23g

Egg & Cheddar Quesadillas
Serves 8

Ingredients
2 Tbsp. grass-fed butter
1 dozen eggs, beaten
1 cup organic salsa of your choice
8 organic large spinach tortillas
1 cup organic sharp cheddar cheese, shredded

Directions
Heat medium pan on low-medium heat and add in butter. Swirl it around to coat surface of pan. Add in beaten eggs and stir until mostly set.
Add in salsa and fold into eggs until firm.
Spoon egg mixture onto 4 tortillas and sprinkle with cheese.
Place remaining tortillas on top.
Sprinkle with cheese then cover with remaining tortillas like a sandwich.
In a separate pan, heat 1 Tbsp. of butter and toast each quesadilla on each side until cheese is melted. Cut into quarters and serve.

Egg & Mushroom Wraps
Serves 6

Ingredients
6 slices turkey bacon, cooked and crumbled
4 oz. mushrooms of your choice (we like button mushrooms)
4 oz. spinach
12 eggs, beaten
1 Tbsp. grass-fed butter

6 Ezekial wraps (or wraps of your choice)

Directions
Heat large pan and butter over medium heat. Add in mushrooms and cook for about 2 minutes. Add in spinach and mix around pan until wilted.
Pour in egg mixture, using a spatula to gently scramble eggs.
Scoop egg mixture into center of each wrap and top each with bacon crumbles. Fold the wrap like a burrito and enjoy!

NUTRITION PER SERVING | **Fats: 38g • Carbohydrates: 58g • Fiber: 14g**
Protein: 39g

Egg Scramble
Serves 1-2

Ingredients
3 whole eggs
1/4 diced red pepper
1/4 diced onion
1 cup mushrooms, sliced
handful spinach leaves
dash of sea salt
1 slice white cheese (optional)
Also:
1/3 avocado, smeared on toast
2 slices toasted bread

Directions
Lightly coat medium sauté pan with grapeseed oil and put on low heat.
Dice peppers and onions and add to pan. Sauté about 2 minutes, then add
mushrooms. Whip eggs in medium mixing bowl.
Once the peppers, onions and mushrooms soften, add spinach leaves.
Once spinach begins to wilt, evenly pour eggs into pan.
Lightly stir into a scramble. Once desired consistency is reached, turn off
stovetop, mix in cheese and serve with toast smeared with avocado.

FOOD FACTOIDS

CRIMINI MUSHROOMS

Crimini mushrooms are a great source for tryptophan, which stimulates the release of serotonin, aiding in better sleep patterns.

NUTRITION PER SERVING | Fats: 41g • Carbohydrates: 74g • Fiber: 16g
Protein: 34g

Eggs, Greens & Bean Burrito
Serves 1

Ingredients
2 eggs
handful spinach
1/3 cup red or black beans
sprinkle of white, sharp cheddar (optional)
3 thin slices avocado (optional)
dash of pepper
Bragg All Natural Herb & Spice Seasoning (optional)
1 tsp. Vegenaise spread (optional)
1 whole wheat or gluten-free wrap

Directions
Scramble eggs, and then mix in beans and seasoning when eggs are almost done. Stir well.
Spread Vegenaise onto wrap.
Grate cheese onto wrap and add cooked eggs and beans.
Top with spinach and sliced avocado.
Wrap up tightly and enjoy!

BREAKFAST

NUTRITION
PER SERVING

**Fats: 24g • Carbohydrates: 13g • Fiber: 3g
Protein: 23g**

Eggs, Veggie & Goat Cheese Casserole
Serves 4

Ingredients
1 red onion, chopped
2 tsp. grapeseed oil
6 oz. baby spinach leaves
10 eggs, lightly beaten
1-2 tsp. Bragg's Seasoning
Pink Himalayan sea salt and fresh ground black pepper to taste
1/2 cup low-fat cottage cheese, rinsed with cold water and drained well
3 oz. soft goat cheese, crumbled

Directions
Preheat oven to 375 degrees.
Measure 1/2 cup low-fat cottage cheese, put in a fine strainer, and rinse with cold water.
Add grapeseed oil to pan on low-medium heat, then add onions and sauté 3 minutes. Add the spinach leaves and sauté 3-4 minutes more. While vegetables are cooking, lightly beat the eggs with Bragg's Seasoning, sea salt and pepper.

Wipe the inside of a 8" x 8" casserole dish with grapeseed oil. Spread spinach/onion mixture in the bottom of the dish, then layer on cottage cheese and goat cheese.

Pour egg mixture over everything. Gently stir so the veggies and cheese are evenly mixed into the eggs.

Bake 20-25 minutes, or until eggs are set and lightly browned.

Cut into pieces and serve warm.

NUTRITION
PER SERVING | **Fats: 44g • Carbohydrates: 20g • Fiber: 4g
Protein: 17g**

Feta, Spinach & Tomato Egg Scramble
Serves 1

Ingredients
2 whole eggs
3-4 Tbsp. almond milk
large handful baby spinach
1 Tbsp. feta
1 small vine-ripened tomato, seeded & diced
2 Tbsp. grapeseed oil
2 Tbsp. red beans (optional)

dash of black pepper

Directions
Heat grapeseed oil in medium pan on low.
Whisk eggs and milk together in small bowl and add to pan, stirring frequently.
When eggs are still a bit runny, add in spinach and beans, and continue mixing.
Spinach will wilt as eggs cook.
Once done, spoon eggs onto small plate and top with diced tomatoes, black pepper and feta.

NUTRITION PER SERVING | Fats: 3g • Carbohydrates: 21g • Fiber: 5g
Protein: 3g

Granola Berry Smash
Serves 1

Ingredients
1/4 cup blueberries
1/4 cup strawberries
1/4 cup granola
splash of unsweetened almond milk

dash of cinnamon

Directions
Warm berries in small pot and put in bowl.
Top with granola and a splash of almond milk. Sprinkle with cinnamon.
Enjoy!

NUTRITION
PER SERVING

Fats: 1g • Carbohydrates: 23g • Fiber: 2g
Protein: 13g

Greek Yogurt Quinoa Cup
Serves 8

Ingredients
1 cup quinoa, cooked according to package directions and cooled
1/4 cup orange blossom honey
1/4 tsp. Pink Himalayan sea salt
4 cups plain low-fat Greek yogurt

2 cups fresh berries of your choice

Directions
Add honey and salt to cooked cold quinoa.
Scoop 1/4 cup Greek yogurt each into a 8 tall glasses. Layer yogurt with 2 Tbsp. quinoa and 2 Tbsp. berries. Repeat layers until cup is full.

NUTRITION
PER SERVING

Fats: 28g • Carbohydrates: 14g • Fiber: 8g
Protein: 15g

Hardboiled Eggs & Avocado Breakfast Salad
Serves 1

Ingredients
2 hard-boiled eggs
1/2 avocado, peeled
sprinkle of pepper
sprinkle of sea salt
dash of paprika

1 tsp. Vegenaise (optional)

Directions
Peel eggs, and then add to small bowl and mash.
Add in avocado and mash with eggs.
Mix in Vegenaise, salt, pepper and paprika.
Mix well and enjoy!

This also goes great on your favorite healthy bread or wrap!

FOOD FACTOIDS · · · · · · · · · · · · · · ·

PINK HIMALAYAN SEA SALT

Pink Himalayan sea salt gets its color from its abundant and varying energy-rich iron content along with 80+ minerals, which are essential for electrolyte balance. It also naturally has iodine and contains less sodium per serving compared to table salt.

BREAKFAST

NUTRITION
PER SERVING

Fats: 4.5g • Carbohydrates: 3g • Fiber: 0g
Protein: 4g

Mini Cheesy Egg Bites
24 mini quiches (in mini-muffin pan)

Ingredients
1/2 cup oat bran
8 eggs
1/2 cup almond milk
dash of Pink Himalayan sea salt
dash of fresh cracked pepper
1 cup shredded organic sharp cheddar cheese
grass-fed butter
mini-muffin cups
mini-muffin pan

Directions
Preheat oven to 350 degrees. With a paper towel, wipe the inside of the muffin cups with butter. Put about 1/2 tsp. of oat bran at the bottom of each cup and tap muffin pan to lightly coat sides of each muffin cup. Whisk eggs, almond milk, salt and pepper together until blended. Then stir in cheddar cheese. Spoon the mixture into the cups.
Bake for about 12 to 15 minutes or until firm. Serve warm.

BREAKFAST

Fats: 19g • Carbohydrates: 58g • Fiber: 7g
Protein: 8g

Oatmeal Breakfast Casserole
Serves 3-4

Ingredients
1/2 cup regular old-fashioned organic oats
2 cups almond milk
1 small sweet potato, peeled and chopped
1 large banana
1 1/2 Tbsp. chia seeds
1 1/2 Tbsp. hemp seeds (optional)
2 tsp. pure vanilla extract
1 tsp. cinnamon
dash of Pink Himalayan sea salt
2 Tbsp. pure maple syrup

Pecan Topping
1/3 cup chopped pecans
2 Tbsp. grass-fed butter
2 Tbsp. almond flour

1/4 cup organic honey (or agave)

Directions

Preheat oven to 350 degrees. Bring 4 cups of water to a boil in a medium sized pot. Add in sweet potato (make sure sweet potato is covered with the water) and cook for about 10 minutes until tender. Drain and set aside.

In same pot, add in the oats, milk, hemp seeds and chia seeds. Stir well and bring to a boil. Reduce heat to a simmer and let cook for about 6 minutes, stirring frequently.

Next, mash in the cooked sweet potato and banana into the pot. Stir in the cinnamon, maple syrup, vanilla and salt to taste. Cook on low for another few minutes.

For the Topping

Mix together the pecans, almond flour, butter and honey with a fork. Pour the oatmeal into an 8" x 8" casserole dish or round cake pan and spread out evenly. Sprinkle on the topping.

Bake until topping browns, about 15 minutes.

Serve warm!

NUTRITION
PER SERVING
| Fats: 3.5g • Carbohydrates: 59g • Fiber: 10g
Protein: 7g

Oats & Berries Smoothie
Serves 1-2

Note: There are more smoothie recipes later in the book!

Ingredients
1 cup blueberries
1 cup strawberries
1 orange
1 banana
1/2 cup uncooked oat bran or buckwheat
1/2 cup almond milk
1 tsp. agave
1 tsp. ground flaxseed

10 ice cubes

Directions
Combine in blender and blend until creamy.

**Fats: 30g • Carbohydrates: 16g • Fiber: 3g
Protein: 28g**

Omelet
Serves 1

Ingredients
3 whole eggs
1/4 diced red pepper
1/4 diced onion
1/4 cup almond milk
1 cup mushrooms, sliced
handful spinach leaves
dash of sea salt
1 slice Havarti cheese (optional)

Directions
Lightly coat 2 medium sauté pans with grapeseed oil and put on low heat.
Dice peppers, onions and mushrooms. Add to pan #1. Sauté for about 2 minutes and add mushrooms.
Whip eggs and milk in medium mixing bowl.
Once the vegetables begin to soften, add spinach leaves to pan #1.
Once spinach has begun to wilt, remove pan #1 from heat.
Evenly pour eggs into pan #2 so they coat the bottom of the pan and cover. (Do not stir.)
Once eggs harden, flip the omelet over and immediately add contents of pan #1 and cheese slice to half of the omelet. Fold the empty omelet half over on top and serve.

NUTRITION
PER SERVING | Fats: 27g • Carbohydrates: 8g • Fiber: 2g
Protein: 15g

Parmesan Pepper Omelet
Serves 1

Ingredients
1/2 chopped green or red bell pepper
dash of Pink Himalayan sea salt and freshly ground pepper
2 eggs
2 tsp. almond milk (or milk of your choice)
1 Tbsp. grass-fed butter
2 tsp. Parmesan, freshly grated

Directions
Add eggs, almond milk, salt and pepper to bowl and whisk together until well blended.
Heat an 8" pan over medium-high heat. Add grapeseed oil.
Add bell peppers to pan and cook until crisp, but tender. Remove peppers and set aside.
Lower heat to low-medium. Add egg mixture.
As the egg turns firm, add peppers to middle of omelet and sprinkle on Parmesan.
Scoop a spatula under one side of the egg pancake and flip over into the other side of the egg to enclose the peppers and Parmesan. Cook for another minute.
Remove omelet with spatula and serve.

NUTRITION
PER SERVING | **Fats: 33g • Carbohydrates: 54g • Fiber: 9g**
Protein: 25g

Peanut Butter & Jelly French Toast
Serves 2

Ingredients
2 eggs
3 Tbsp. almond milk
4 slices toasted whole wheat or gluten-free bread
1/2 cup finely chopped peanuts
1 Tbsp. grass-fed butter
organic fruit spread or maple syrup

Directions
Beat eggs and milk together. Dip 1 bread slice at a time in egg mixture, turning once; dip each slice into peanuts to coat both sides.
Heat butter in pan over low-medium heat. Place as many bread slices as fits in pan and cook until brown on each side.
Serve with organic fruit spread or warm maple syrup.

Pitbull Pancakes
Serves 4-6

Ingredients
1 cup Pamela's Baking & Pancake Mix (or similar brown rice mix)
1 large egg or egg alternative*
3/4 cup water
1 Tbsp. coconut oil

Directions
Follow the pancake directions on the back of the mix.
Use coconut oil for the mix and to cook the pancakes.
Serve with Fresh Berry Syrup.

Note: Add more water to batter for thinner pancakes. Less water for thicker pancakes.

*EASY EGG ALTERNATIVE (This egg substitution is equal to 1 egg.)
1 Tbsp. ground flax seeds
3 Tbsp. water
Stir together until thick and gelatinous.

NUTRITION PER SERVING | **Fats: 0g • Carbohydrates: 13g • Fiber: 2g**
Protein: 1g

Fresh Berry Syrup
Serves 4-6

Note: Pairs with pancakes, East Coast Breakfast Toast, plain Greek yogurt, cereals & more!

Ingredients
4 oz. water
1 cup strawberries
1 cup blueberries
1 Tbsp. agave or honey (optional)

Directions
Add water and fruit to small saucepan.
Cover and turn to low-medium heat.
When fruit softens, reduce heat and mash with spatula.
Add agave or honey, stir and serve.

NUTRITION PER SERVING | Fat: 10g • Carbohydrates: 70g • Fiber: 13g
Protein: 14

Pumpkin Oatmeal Breakfast
Serves 1

Ingredients
1 3/4 cups almond milk (or milk of your choice)
1/2 cup uncooked organic quick oats
1/2 cup canned organic pumpkin puree
1/2 tsp. pumpkin pie spice
dash of Pink Himalayan sea salt
drizzle of honey or agave

Directions
In a small pot, bring almond milk and oats to a boil. Mix in canned pumpkin and pumpkin spice. Reduce heat to simmer. Keep stirring until oats are cooked. Serve with a drizzle of honey or agave.

NUTRITION PER SERVING | Fats: 12g • Carbohydrates: 35g • Fiber: 4g
Protein: 4g

Pumpkin Spice Quinoa Bake
Serves 4

Ingredients
2/3 cup warm water
1 banana
2 Tbsp. organic pumpkin puree
1 Tbsp. maple syrup
1 tsp. coconut oil, melted
1/4 tsp. pure organic vanilla extract
1 tsp. pumpkin pie spice
1/4 cup raw quinoa

For The Topping
1/4 cup raisins
1/4 cup raw pecans, chopped
2 Tbsp. almond flour
2 Tbsp. maple syrup
1 Tbsp. coconut flour
1/2 tsp. cinnamon
1/2 tsp. nutmeg
sprinkle of sea salt

1 Tbsp. coconut oil

Directions

Preheat oven to 350 degrees.

Mash banana in bowl first.

Add banana, water, pumpkin puree, maple syrup, coconut oil, vanilla and pumpkin pie spice to an 8" x 8" casserole dish or round cake pan. Stir to combine. Then add quinoa.

Cover with glass lid or foil and bake for 45 minutes, or until most of the liquid is gone.

While the casserole is cooking, let's work on the topping.

Add pecans, raisins, almond flour, maple syrup, coconut flour, cinnamon, nutmeg and salt to a small bowl. Mix well, then stir in coconut oil. Put the bowl in the freezer.

Once casserole is done, remove it from the oven, take off the cover and top with the crumbled topping. Then bake uncovered for about 12 minutes, or until topping browns.

NUTRITION
PER SERVING | Fats: 26g • Carbohydrates: 49g • Fiber: 10g
Protein: 23g

Oatmeal & Soft-Cooked Egg
Serves 1

Ingredients
1/2 cup organic oat bran
dash of Pink Himalayan sea salt and pepper
1 egg
2 Tbsp. sharp cheddar, shredded
1 tsp. grass-fed butter

Directions
Bring 1 cup water to a boil in a small pot. Add oat bran and salt, reduce heat to a simmer and cook until soft. Heat 1 tsp. grass-fed butter in a small pan over medium heat. Add whole egg (without breaking yolk) and cook about 3 minutes. Season egg to taste with salt and pepper. Serve oatmeal in a bowl topped with cheese and egg.

Fats: 18g • Carbohydrates: 30g • Fiber: 3g
Protein: 10g

Scrambled Egg Pancake Sammies
Serves 4 (8 pancakes)

Ingredients
4 eggs
1/4 cup almond milk (or milk of your choice)
dash of Pink Himalayan sea salt
dash of pepper
2 tsp. grass-fed butter
16 silver dollar-size Pitbull pancakes* (about 3 inches in diameter), pre-made
warm maple syrup to drizzle on top
*See recipe for Pitbull pancakes in Breakfast section

Directions
Whisk eggs, almond milk, salt and pepper in a bowl.
Add butter to medium pan, on low-medium heat. Pour in egg mixture and scramble, stirring occasionally until eggs are set.
Spoon eggs onto 8 pancakes, dividing evenly. Top with remaining pancakes. Drizzle with maple syrup.

NUTRITION
PER SERVING | **Fats: 41g • Carbohydrates: 33g • Fiber: 5g**
Protein: 29g

Spinach, Bell Pepper & Mushroom Frittata
Serves 2-4

Ingredients
2 Tbsp. grapeseed oil
8 eggs
1/2 cup almond milk
2 garlic cloves, minced
2 cups baby spinach, chopped
1 sweet onion, chopped
1 green bell pepper, chopped
5 oz. crimini mushrooms
sea salt, to taste
black pepper, to taste
ketchup, for dipping (optional)

Directions
Heat large pan with grapeseed oil and add garlic, spinach, onion, mushrooms and green pepper.
Cook about 4 minutes or until vegetables are tender.
In a small bowl, mix eggs and milk and add to vegetable pan, reduce heat to a simmer and cover.
Cook about 8 minutes.
Cut into wedges and serve.

NUTRITION PER SERVING | **Fats: 3g • Carbohydrates: 36g • Fiber: 36g**
Protein: 7g

Steel Cut Oats & Dates
Serves 1-2

Ingredients
1/4 cup steel cut oats
3/4 cup water or almond milk
dash of cinnamon
1/4 cup chopped dates

Directions
Bring water to a boil.
Add oats, dates and dash of cinnamon and then simmer for about 20 minutes.
Remove from heat and let stand for 2-3 minutes before serving.

Tater Tots
Serves 4-6

Note: Serve these breakfast potatoes with your favorite egg recipe.

Ingredients
8 red potatoes, cut into bite-sized pieces
1/4 bell pepper, diced
1/2 onion, chopped
2 cloves garlic, chopped
2 Tbsp. grapeseed oil
Sea salt, to taste
Black pepper, to taste

Directions
In large pan, heat grapeseed oil on medium and add potatoes, mixing frequently.
When potatoes begin to brown, add in onion, bell pepper and garlic and continue
mixing about another 10 minutes until potatoes are tender.
Sprinkle with salt and pepper.
Serve hot.

BREAKFAST

NUTRITION PER SERVING | Fats: 12g • Carbohydrates: 23g • Fiber: 8g
Protein: 30g

Tofu & Kale Scramble
Serves 2-4

Ingredients
1 green bell pepper, diced
8 oz. mushrooms, sliced
2 cloves garlic, minced
15 oz. of tofu, firm or extra-firm, crumbled
1 1/2 tsp. smoked paprika
1 tsp. ground cumin
sea salt, to taste
dash of turmeric
handful kale
1/4 cup nutritional yeast

Directions
Sauté mushrooms, pepper and garlic in grapeseed oil on medium heat until tender.
Add the tofu, stirring often. Add the spices followed by the kale.
Add a tsp. of water, cover and steam, stirring every minute or so, until the kale wilts.
Mix in the nutritional yeast and cook for 2 more minutes until hot throughout.
Serve and enjoy!

**Fats: 13g • Carbohydrates: 9g • Fiber: 3g
Protein: 20g**

Tofu Veggie Scramble
Serves 4-6

Ingredients
2 (15 oz.) packages firm tofu
1 Tbsp. grapeseed oil
3 green onions, chopped
3 garlic cloves, minced
1 Tbsp. fresh squeezed lime juice
1/2 green bell pepper, chopped
1/2 red bell pepper, chopped
4 sprays of Bragg Liquid Aminos (or 2 Tbsp. low-sodium soy sauce)
3/4 cup salsa (see homemade recipe for salsa in Snack section)
1/4 cup cilantro, chopped
dash of black pepper, to taste

Directions
Drain tofu, pat dry and grate into large bowl.
In large pan, sauté onions, garlic and bell peppers on medium heat in grapeseed oil until tender. Mix in the grated tofu and cook another 5 minutes, stirring often.
Now add in lime juice, Bragg Liquid Aminos, salsa and cilantro and mix well.
Serve over leafy greens, or whole wheat or gluten-free toast.

LUNCH

LUNCH

NUTRITION PER SERVING

Fats: 29g • Carbohydrates: 76g • Fiber: 11g
Protein: 8g

Apple, Raisin & Carrot Jubilee
Serves 2

Ingredients
3 large carrots, grated
1/2 cup chopped cashews (put them in a Ziploc bag & smash them with a
meat mallet)
2 apples, cubed
1/2 cup raisins
1 Tbsp. lemon juice
2 Tbsp. Vegenaise
dash of sea salt
dash of black pepper
1 Tbsp. olive oil

Directions
Put ingredients in a big bowl and mix well. Serve and enjoy!

NUTRITION
PER SERVING

Fats: 17g • Carbohydrates: 45g • Fiber: 7g
Protein: 15g

Bacon, Spinach & Tomato Sandwich
Serves 1

Ingredients
2 slices of whole wheat or gluten-free bread
2 slices low-sodium turkey bacon
small handful of fresh spinach leaves
1/2 vine-ripe tomato, thinly sliced
1 Tbsp. Vegenaise

Directions
Cook turkey bacon in a pan with grapeseed oil until crispy, then place on paper towels. Once cool enough, break each bacon piece in half and set aside.
Lightly toast bread, then smear with Vegenaise.
Place tomato slices, followed by spinach then bacon pieces on one bread slice and top with remaining piece of bread.
Cut in half or quarters and enjoy!

NUTRITION
PER SERVING | **Fats: 22g • Carbohydrates: 84g • Fiber: 15g
Protein: 24g**

Bean-tastic Pasta Salad
Serves 6

Ingredients
salt and pepper
6 oz. small pasta noodles (like orecchiette or small shells)
3/4 lb. fresh green beans, trimmed and cut into thirds
2 Tbsp. yellow or Dijon mustard
1/3 cup red-wine vinegar
2 Tbsp. honey
1/2 cup extra-virgin olive oil
1 can (15.5 oz.) pinto beans, rinsed and drained
1 can (15.5 oz.) chickpeas, rinsed and drained
4 scallions (white parts only), thinly sliced
5 stalks celery, chopped

Directions
In a large pot of boiling salted water, cook pasta so it's al dente (cooked enough to be firm but not soft). Add green beans and cook 4 minutes more. Drain and rinse with cold water.

In a medium bowl, combine mustard, vinegar, honey and olive oil. Add pasta mixture, pinto beans, chickpeas, scallions and celery; toss gently. Season with salt and pepper.

Fats: 17g • Carbohydrates: 56g • Fiber: 11g
Protein: 19g

Black Bean & Zucchini Quesadillas
Serves 2

Ingredients
1/2 cup canned black beans, rinsed & drained
2 Tbsp. salsa (Fresh Salsa recipe is in the Sides & Snacks section)
1/2 cup zucchini, peeled & finely chopped
4 whole wheat or gluten-free wraps
1/4 cup aged cheddar cheese (optional)

Directions
Preheat oven to 350 degrees.
Combine beans and salsa in a small bowl; mash with a fork and then mix in zucchini.
Layer 1 wrap with half the bean mixture, sprinkle with some cheese, and then top with another wrap.
Repeat this process with the remaining wraps.
Place wraps on a baking sheet and cook for about 2 minutes on each side until the cheese is melted and wraps are lightly browned.
Enjoy!

NUTRITION
PER SERVING | Fat: 11g • Carbohydrates: 61g • Fiber 10g
Protein: 30g

Brandy's Mom's Macaroni Tuna Salad
Serves 6

Ingredients
16 oz. large whole grain shell pasta
2 cans of organic tuna fish
1 red pepper, diced
1 green pepper, diced
1 onion, diced
1/4 cup mustard seed
Pink Himalayan sea salt, to taste
freshly ground black pepper, to taste
ground garlic powder, to taste
2-3 Tbsp. Vegenaise

Directions
Make pasta according to package directions.
Drain and rinse with cold water to cool.
Mix all ingredients together in large bowl with pasta.

Add spices to taste. Enjoy!

NUTRITION
PER SERVING

**Fats: 21g • Carbohydrates: 31g • Fiber: 7g
Protein: 11g**

Cashew & Mint Quinoa
Serves 4-6

Ingredients
1 cup quinoa
1 cup cashews, crushed
2 Tbsp. extra virgin olive oil
1/2 cup black beans
1/2 cup chickpeas
1/2 cup scallions, chopped
1/4 cup mint, chopped
1 cup cauliflower, finely chopped
1/2 cup carrots, finely chopped

Directions
Cook quinoa according to package directions and set aside.
Sauté carrots and cauliflower until tender.
Combine all ingredients in large bowl and serve.

NUTRITION PER SERVING | Fats: 11g • Carbohydrates: 67g • Fiber: 14g
Protein: 35g

Chicken Apple Quesadillas
Serves 2-4

Ingredients
4 gluten-free tortillas
1 chicken breast, cooked & shredded
1 cup aged white cheddar (optional) or nutritional yeast
1 apple, sliced thin

Directions
In large pan, warm one tortilla at a time, sprinkle each with cheese a scoop of shredded chicken and a thin layer of apples.
Fold tortilla in half and flip over to cook other side.
When cheese melts remove from pan and cut in triangles.

NUTRITION PER SERVING | Fats: 16g • Carbohydrates: 8g • Fiber: 4g
Protein: 33g

Chicken BLT Salad
Serves 2

Ingredients
1 lb. chicken breast, cooked and thinly sliced
1 beefsteak or heirloom tomato, cut into wedges
1 package romaine lettuce
3 turkey bacon slices, cooked and crumbled
1 avocado, chopped into bite-sized pieces
drizzle of olive oil and balsamic vinegar

Directions
Combine first 3 ingredients in a large bowl; toss well.
Put into serving bowls. Drizzle with olive oil and balsamic vinegar. Top with avocado and bacon crumbles.

NUTRITION
PER SERVING

**Fats: 54g • Carbohydrates: 37g • Fiber: 9g
Protein: 19g**

Chickpea Salad
Serves 2

Ingredients
6 oz. chickpeas (garbanzo beans)
handful baby spinach
handful kale
1/2 cucumber, sliced
1/4 chopped onion
1/2 tomato, chopped (or 6 cherry tomatoes)
1/2 cup chopped walnuts
6 sliced strawberries
4 oz. feta cheese crumbles (optional)
3 Tbsp. extra virgin olive oil
3 Tbsp. balsamic vinegar

Directions
Combine all ingredients in bowl and drizzle with olive oil and balsamic
vinegar.

NUTRITION PER SERVING | Fats: 18g • Carbohydrates: 75g • Fiber: 11g
Protein: 24g

Chipotle Veggie Burritos
Serves 3-6

Ingredients
1 Tbsp. grapeseed oil
1 garlic clove, minced
1/2 tsp. chipotle chile powder (Spicely Organics makes one)
1/4 tsp. Pink Himalayan sea salt
1/3 cup water
1 (15 oz.) can organic black beans, drained
1 (15 oz.) can organic pinto beans, drained
3 Tbsp. organic fresh salsa of your choice
6 large Ezekial Sprouted Grain tortillas
1 cup (4 oz.) shredded sharp cheddar cheese
1 1/2 cups beefsteak tomatoes, chopped
2 cups finely chopped baby spinach leaves
6 Tbsp. thinly sliced green onions
6 Tbsp. low-fat Greek yogurt

Directions
Heat grapeseed oil in a large pan over medium heat. Add garlic to pan; cook
1 minute, stirring often. Stir in chipotle chile powder and salt,
water and beans. Bring to a boil, then simmer 10 minutes.

Remove from heat and stir in salsa. Mash some of the bean mixture with a fork. Warm tortillas according to package directions. Spoon a little bean mixture, cheese, tomato, spinach, onions and yogurt. Roll it up and enjoy!

NUTRITION
PER SERVING

Fats: 20g • Carbohydrates: 93g • Fiber: 12g
Protein: 13g

Cinnamon Apple Grilled Cheese
Serves 1

Ingredients
2 slices whole wheat or gluten-free bread
1 organic red apple, thinly sliced
2 Tbsp. maple syrup (agave also works well here)
dash of cinnamon
1 Tbsp. grapeseed oil
2 Tbsp. feta cheese crumbles

Directions
Lightly coat small pan with grapeseed oil and put on medium heat.
Place apple slices in pan. Apples can be touching but not on top of each other.
Drizzle small amount of maple syrup on each slice (not more than 2 Tbsp. worth for the whole pan) and then dash with cinnamon.
Cook for about 2 minutes, then flip and cook for additional 2 minutes until lightly browned around edges.
When apples are almost done, lightly toast bread slices.
Place apples on one side of bread, followed by a layer of feta crumbles and then another layer of hot apple slices. Top with remaining bread slice. Enjoy!

NUTRITION PER SERVING | **Fats: 26g • Carbohydrates: 43g • Fiber: 4g**
Protein: 7g

Cranberry Cashew Spinach Salad
Serves 2-4

Ingredients
3 large handfuls organic spinach (about 3-4 oz.)
1 shallot, chopped
1/4 cup balsamic vinegar
1/4 cup extra virgin olive oil
dash of sea salt
dash of black pepper
1 Tbsp. spicy brown or Dijon mustard
1 cup dried cranberries
1 cup cashews, crushed or whole

Directions
For the dressing, whisk together the chopped shallot pieces, mustard, balsamic vinegar, sea salt and pepper.
Then toss the spinach leaves with dressing and mix in the cranberries and pecans.
Enjoy!

NUTRITION PER SERVING | **Fats: 18g • Carbohydrates: 44g • Fiber: 8g**
Protein: 8g

Cranberry Kale Salad
Serves 4

Ingredients
1/2 large head of kale washed and dried
1 cup red onion, finely chopped
1/2 red bell pepper
2 carrots, chopped
1 cucumber, chopped
1 avocado, chopped
handful of cherry tomatoes
1 cup dried cranberries (no sugar added)
1/4 cup hemp seed
1/3 cup chopped walnuts (or nuts of your choice)

Dressing
drizzle of extra virgin olive oil and balsamic vinegar

Directions
Add chopped vegetables and toss in a large bowl. Tear kale into bite-sized pieces.
Mix vegetables and kale in large bowl. Divide into serving bowls.
Top with hemp seeds, walnuts and cranberries. Drizzle with extra virgin olive oil
and balsamic vinegar.

LUNCH

NUTRITION PER SERVING | **Fats: 39g • Carbohydrates: 113g • Fiber: 9g
Protein: 33g**

Dolce Feta Pizza
Serves 2

Ingredients
1 gluten-free or whole wheat pizza crust
handful kale
1 small onion, chopped
1 15 oz. can diced tomatoes
2 Tbsp. grapeseed oil
dash of Italian herb seasoning
1 cup feta cheese crumbles

Directions
Preheat oven to 350 degrees.
Sauté onions in grapeseed oil until tender.
Add in handful of kale and mix with onions until wilted.
Spread diced tomatoes and their juices over pizza crust, careful to leave the edge of the crust plain.
Spread onion and kale mixture.
Sprinkle feta crumbles evenly over pizza.
Sprinkle on herb seasoning.
Cook for 30 minutes, or until edges of pizza crust brown.
Enjoy!

FOOD | FACTOIDS

GRAPESEED OIL

Have any swelling (edema) in your body, especially if you're pregnant? Grapeseed oil can help reduce that. This is a great remedy for athletes who may experience some swelling after a sports-related injury.

NUTRITION PER SERVING | Fats: 6g • Carbohydrates: 67g • Fiber: 28g
Protein: 22g

Easy Lentil Soup
Serves 4-6

Ingredients
2 Tbsp. grapeseed oil
1 medium onion, finely diced
1 large carrot, peeled and finely diced
2 stalks celery, finely diced
2 medium cloves garlic, minced
1 lb. dried brown lentils
1/2 cup pearl barley
1 bay leaf
2 quarts vegetable broth
dash of Pink Himalayan sea salt
1 Tbsp. fresh lemon juice
1/2 cup chopped parsley
freshly ground black pepper

Directions
Heat grapeseed oil in a large stock pot over medium-high heat for about 1 minute. Add onions, carrots and celery, and cook about 5 minutes, stirring occasionally, until softened. Add garlic and cook about 30 seconds. Add lentils and barley and stir to combine. Add bay leaf,

broth and a dash of sea salt. Bring to a boil, reduce to a simmer, cover with lid slightly cracked, and cook until lentils are completely tender and falling apart, about 1 hour, adding water as necessary. Lentils and barley should be totally covered with water at all times.

Using a hand blender, blend soup until as smooth as desired. Whisk in lemon juice to taste, along with parsley. Season to taste with salt and pepper and serve.

LUNCH

NUTRITION PER SERVING	Fats: 25g • Carbohydrates: 25g • Fiber: 9g Protein: 16g

Egg Salad
Serves 2

Ingredients
4 whole hard-boiled eggs, peeled & chopped
1/4 onion, chopped
1 celery stalk, chopped
dash sea salt
dash black pepper
1 avocado
bread or wrap

Directions
Combine eggs, onion, celery, salt and pepper in mixing bowl. Scoop out whole avocado and add to mixture. Mash well. Serve on whole wheat or gluten-free bread, in wrap or over salad.

Fats: 26g • Carbohydrates: 59g • Fiber: 9g
Protein: 26g

THE G.O.A.T. Cheese Pizza
Serves 4

Ingredients
2 Ezekiel sprouted grain tortillas, thawed
1 garlic clove, minced
1 cup shredded baby spinach leaves
2-3 plum tomatoes, chopped
2 oz. mozzarella cheese, shredded
3 oz. goat cheese, crumbled

Directions
Preheat oven to 450 degrees.
Place tortillas on large baking sheet and put in oven, about 4 minutes.
Once tortilla has started to slightly crisp on edges, remove from oven.
Sprinkle garlic, tomato, cheeses and spinach around each tortilla. Place back in oven until crust edges are browned and cheese is melted. Serve immediately.

NUTRITION PER SERVING | **Fats: 9g • Carbohydrates: 18g • Fiber: 4g Protein: 11g**

Grape Green Salad With Eggs
Serves 4

Ingredients
1 small package organic baby spinach (9 oz.)
1-2 large Heirloom tomatoes, sliced (or tomatoes of your choice)
4 hard-boiled eggs, cut into wedges
1/2 cup feta cheese crumbles
3/4 cup red grapes, halved
drizzle of olive oil

Directions
Divide spinach, tomatoes and grapes among serving bowls. Top with egg wedges. Sprinkle with cheese. Drizzle with olive oil.

NUTRITION PER SERVING

Fats: 12g • Carbohydrates: 51g • Fiber: 8g
Protein: 45g

Greek Yogurt Chicken Salad Sandwich
Serves 4

Ingredients
1 lb. cooked chicken breast, shredded
1/2 cup red onion, chopped
1/2 cup apple, chopped
3/4 cup red grapes, halved
1/4 cup almonds, chopped
1/2 cup plain Greek yogurt
1 Tbsp. freshly squeezed lemon juice, to taste
dash of Pink Himalayan sea salt and black pepper
8 slices whole wheat or gluten-free bread

Directions
In a large bowl, combine chicken, red onion, apple, grapes, almonds, Greek yogurt, lemon juice, salt and pepper, to taste. Put mixture on 4 bread slices. Top each with 4 remaining bread slices. Cut each sandwich in half. Enjoy!

LUNCH

NUTRITION
PER SERVING

**Fats: 96g • Carbohydrates: 65g • Fiber: 14g
Protein: 28g**

The Green Reuben
Serves 1

Ingredients
Reuben Dressing (recipe follows - make this first)
2 slices whole wheat or gluten-free bread
1 Tbsp. mustard
1/4 cup Eden Organic Sauerkraut (or similar)
2 slices of Swiss cheese
1/2 avocado
2 Tbsp. grapeseed oil

Directions
Spread one slice of bread with some mustard, the other slice with
Reuben Dressing.
Drizzle grapeseed oil into, and then add in bread slices, dry side down.
Top one slice with avocado and Swiss cheese, and the other with
sauerkraut.
Over medium heat, grill the sandwich until browned, about 5 minutes.
Put the sandwich halves together and enjoy!

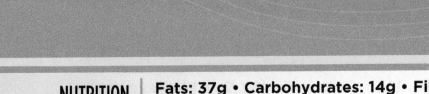

NUTRITION PER SERVING | **Fats: 37g • Carbohydrates: 14g • Fiber: 1g Protein: 1g**

Reuben Dressing
Serves 1

Ingredients
4 Tbsp. Vegenaise
1 1/2 Tbsp. ketchup
1 Tbsp. horseradish
1/2 tsp. sweet pickle relish
dash of Worcestershire sauce

Directions
Blend the ingredients thoroughly in a bowl.
Spread on bread slice to complete your Green Reuben.
Enjoy!

NUTRITION PER SERVING | **Fats: 18g • Carbohydrates: 9g • Fiber: 2g**
Protein: 6g

Heirloom Tomato & Burrata Cheese Salad
Serves 4

Ingredients
4 large heirloom tomatoes (about 2 1/2 lbs.) or 4 to 5 large plum tomatoes
1 cup cherry tomatoes, halved
dash of Pink Himalayan sea salt
freshly ground black pepper
1 tsp. dried oregano
1/4 cup torn fresh basil leaves
1/4 cup extra-virgin olive oil
4 (2.5 oz.) rounds burrata cheese (or fresh mozzarella)

Directions
Cut tomatoes into wedges and place in large bowl along with cherry tomato halves. Sprinkle with sea salt and pepper. Sprinkle on oregano.
Add 1/4 cup basil and olive oil and mix well. Let stand at room temperature at least 30 minutes and up to 1 hour, stirring occasionally.

Place 1 burrata cheese round in center of each plate. Fan tomatoes around cheese, dividing equally. Drizzle with dressing from bowl.
Garnish with additional basil leaves and serve.

BASIL

Feeling constipated, nauseous or have a headache?
Basil is a great, natural remedy to ease all
three ailments.

NUTRITION PER SERVING | Fats: 16g • Carbohydrates: 41g • Fiber: 3g
Protein: 17g

Homemade Refried Bean Tacos
Serves 4-6

Ingredients
1 15 oz. can pinto beans, drained
1/2 cup aged cheddar, shredded (optional)
dash of sea salt
6 organic taco shells (choose gluten-free shells if you'd like)
splash of water
1 small onion, diced
large handful of spinach, shredded
2 small tomatoes, diced

Directions
In small pan, sauté onions until tender.
In small pot add pinto beans, onions, splash of water, dash of sea salt and a sprinkle of the cheddar cheese and put on low heat.
Mash bean mixture with potato masher or fork, and crush and mix until smooth. (You can also use an electric mixer or food processor here and then add the mixture to the pot to warm.)
Once smooth and heated, spoon beans into taco shells.
Top with spinach, tomato and leftover shredded cheese.

NUTRITION
PER SERVING | Fats: 22g • Carbohydrates: 42g • Fiber: 4g
Protein: 27g

Honey Chicken Lettuce Cups
Serves 4-6

Ingredients
10 large butter lettuce leaves
8-10 sprays of Bragg Liquid Aminos to taste (or 2 Tbsp. low-sodium soy sauce)
3 Tbsp. honey
2 Tbsp. apple cider vinegar
4 Tbsp. peanut oil
3 boneless skinless chicken breasts, chopped
dash of black pepper
2 garlic cloves, finely chopped
1 Tbsp. ginger root, grated
1 bunch scallions, diced
8 oz. water chestnuts, drained
1/4 cup roasted unsalted cashews, crushed
1 tsp. sesame seeds
1 cup quinoa (optional)

Directions
Sprinkle the chicken pieces with pepper and cook it in the peanut oil on medium to high heat, stirring occasionally.

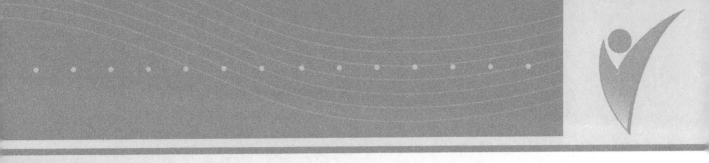

Add 2 Tbsp. peanut oil to separate large pan and stir in the grated ginger, garlic and scallions.

In about 2 minutes, add in water chestnuts, cashews and the honey mixture. Sauté together for about 2-3 minutes and then reduce to a simmer.

Once the chicken is done, drain juices from pan and add the chicken to the veggie pan. Mix everything together thoroughly. Remove from heat.

Put mixture in serving bowl and the lettuce leaves on a plate. To serve, spoon the chicken into each lettuce leaf, wrap the leaf around the chicken mixture, and enjoy!

NUTRITION
PER SERVING

Fats: 31g • Carbohydrates: 24g • Fiber: 4g
Protein: 27g

Honey Mustard Turkey & Pear Salad
Serves 2-4

Ingredients
1 organic turkey breast (not deli slices)
2 large handfuls arugula & spinach mix
1 pear, sliced into thin, flat pieces
1 Tbsp. apple cider vinegar
3 Tbsp. extra virgin olive oil
1 Tbsp. feta crumbles or 2 slices provolone (optional)
1 Tbsp. Annie's Organic Honey Mustard (or similar)

Directions
Slice raw turkey breast and brush with honey mustard. Cook in pan with grapeseed oil.
Layer pear slices on turkey pieces in pan. Follow with layer of cheese.
Cover and cook about 3 minutes until cheese melts.
Place spinach and arugula mix into bowls and place turkey slices on top.
Dressing: Whisk a Tbsp. of the honey mustard with a Tbsp. of olive oil and drizzle onto salad.

Honey, Yam & Bean Wrap
Serves 4-6

Ingredients
8 whole wheat or gluten-free wraps
2 large yams, peeled & cut into chunks
4 Tbsp. grapeseed oil
1/2 yellow onion, diced
2 cups cooked black beans, rinsed & drained
1/2 tsp. ground cumin
dash of sea salt, to taste
dash of black pepper, to taste
drizzle of honey

Directions
Preheat oven to 375 degrees.
In large mixing bowl, toss yam chunks with 3 Tbsp. of grapeseed oil.
Spread coated yams on baking sheet and cook for 20 minutes or until tender.
In large pan, add 1 Tbsp. grapeseed oil and sauté onion until tender.
Add beans, cumin, salt and pepper to onion pan and stir well.
Remove from heat and mix in cooked yams.
Spoon mixture into wraps, drizzle with honey, fold up and enjoy!

NUTRITION
PER SERVING

Fats: 63g • Carbohydrates: 46g • Fiber: 11g
Protein: 47g

Hot Avocado Chicken Sandwich
Serves 1

Ingredients
2 slices whole wheat or gluten-free bread
1 slice cheddar, or cheese of your choice
1 chicken breast, cooked & chopped
1 Tbsp. green pepper, minced
1 Tbsp. onion, minced
1 Tbsp. Vegenaise
3 thin avocado slices
2 Tbsp. grapeseed oil (for sautéing)

Directions
Chop chicken, peppers and onions and sauté in separate pans in grapeseed oil. (Chicken in one pan, veggies in the other.)
Make sure to cook onions and green peppers until soft.
Slice avocado pieces and set aside.
When chicken and veggies are nearly done, toast your bread.
As soon as bread is done, spread Vegenaise onto slices, then lay down the avocado, then cheese and top with hot chicken and veggies. Top with other bread slice, mash down and enjoy!

FOOD | FACTOIDS

YELLOW ONION

Feeling a little under the weather? Add some yellow onion to your soup as it has antioxidant and immune-boosting properties.

NUTRITION
PER SERVING | **Fats: 12g • Carbohydrates: 12g • Fiber: 3g
Protein: 47g**

Italian Chicken Kabobs
Serves 4-6

Ingredients
1 1/2 lbs. skinless boneless chicken breast, cut into 2-inch chunks
12 skewers
2 Tbsp. apple cider vinegar
1 1/2 tsp. sea salt
1/2 tsp. hot red pepper flakes (optional)
1 Tbsp. extra virgin olive oil
1 Tbsp. fresh basil, chopped
1 Tbsp. fresh oregano, chopped
2 garlic cloves, minced
2 zucchini, sliced into rounds
1 large red bell pepper, seeded & cut into 2-inch slices
1 large green bell pepper, seeded & cut into 2-inch slices
7 oz. Portabella mushrooms, cut into chunks (optional)

Directions
The key to the kabob is cut everything so that you can spear it with a stick!
You can make this on the grill or in the oven. If using oven, preheat to 350
degrees.

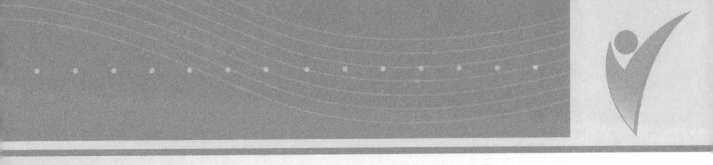

Whisk apple cider vinegar, 1 tsp. sea salt, and hot red pepper in bowl, followed by olive oil. Add basil, oregano and garlic, and stir. Add in chicken and toss to coat. Let marinate about 15-20 minutes.

In large pan, sear all sides of the chicken pieces so that when skewered, no raw chicken is touching the veggies.

Skewer the chicken and all veggies and place on grill, turning occasionally until chicken is cooked through and veggies are browned at edges. If cooking in oven, you'll need one large (or multiple) baking dish(es).

Place skewers in baking dishes, brush chicken and veggies with sauce and cook for about 30 minutes or until chicken pieces are cooked through and veggies are browned at edges.

Whether you're cooking these on the grill or in the oven, be sure to baste occasionally while cooking. Serve and enjoy!

NUTRITION
PER SERVING | **Fats: 8g • Carbohydrates: 61g • Fiber: 2g**
Protein: 45g

Maple Chicken Veggie Kabobs
Serves 4-6

Ingredients
1 1/2 lbs. skinless boneless chicken breast, cut into 2-inch chunks
12 skewers
1 tsp. sea salt
1 large red bell pepper, seeded & cut into 2-inch slices
1 large green bell pepper, seeded & cut into 2-inch slices
7 oz. Portabella mushrooms, cut into chunks (optional)
1 bottle Annie's Organic Smoky Maple BBQ Sauce (or similar)

Directions
The key to the kabob is to cut everything so that you can spear it with a stick!
You can make this on the grill or in the oven. If using oven, preheat to 350 degrees.
In bowl, coat chicken chunks with about 3/4 cup of the Annie's Maple BBQ Sauce, cover and let marinate about 15-20 minutes.
Then, in large pan, sear all sides of the chicken pieces so that when skewered, no raw chicken is touching the veggies.

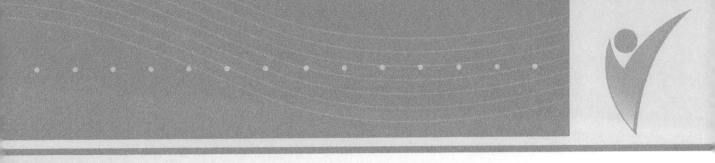

Skewer the chicken and all veggies and place on grill, turning occasionally until chicken is cooked through and veggies are browned at edges. If cooking in oven, you'll need one large (or multiple) baking dish(es).

Place skewers in baking dishes, brush chicken and veggies with sauce and cook for about 30 minutes or until chicken pieces are cooked through and veggies are browned at edges.

Whether you're cooking these on the grill or in the oven, be sure to baste occasionally while cooking.

NUTRITION
PER SERVING | Fats: 17g • Carbohydrates: 25g • Fiber: 6g
Protein: 33g

Mike's Avocado Salmon Salad
Serves 2-4

Ingredients
1 6-oz. can wild-caught Alaskan Sockeye
1/2 stalk celery, chopped
1/4 cup red or sweet onion, chopped
2 tsp. spicy brown mustard or horseradish
2 Tbsp. dill pickle relish (unsweetened)
1/4 tsp. black pepper
7 pitted black olives, chopped (optional)
1/2 avocado
brown rice wrap or bread

Directions
Put salmon in a large mixing bowl and mix in celery, onion, mustard, relish, olives, pepper and avocado. Mix thoroughly, stirring avocado into the mixture. Transfer salad to brown rice wrap or bread. Enjoy!

NUTRITION PER SERVING | **Fats: 23g • Carbohydrates: 70g • Fiber: 11g**
Protein: 43g

Open-Face Turkey Salad Sandwich
Serves 4

Ingredients
8 slices whole wheat or gluten-free bread, lightly toasted
2 fresh turkey breasts (not deli slices)
2 Tbsp. olive oil
2 cups seedless red grapes, halved
2 apples, chopped
6 cups fresh baby spinach
2 Tbsp. apple cider vinegar
4 pieces provolone, thinly sliced

Directions
Thinly slice turkey breast and cook in grapeseed oil. Layer provolone slice over turkey breast, then set aside.
In pan, lightly sauté grapes and apples in grapeseed oil for about 1-2 minutes.
Place two pieces of bread on a plate and layer with turkey slices, apple and grape mixture, spinach and drizzle with apple cider vinegar.

LUNCH

NUTRITION PER SERVING | **Fats: 7g • Carbohydrates: 65g • Fiber: 8g Protein: 21g**

Pasta Salad With Veggies
Serves 2-4

Ingredients
2 cups rotini pasta or gluten-free pasta, cooked according to package instructions & drained
1 cup chopped broccoli, steamed
1 cup chickpeas
1/3 cup cubed or shredded mozzarella cheese (optional)
1 clove garlic, minced
1/2 tomato, diced

Dressing
light drizzle of extra virgin olive oil & balsamic vinegar

Directions
In a bowl, mix all ingredients together. Cool in refrigerator until ready to serve. To serve, add dressing and cheese.

NUTRITION PER SERVING | **Fats: 37g** • **Carbohydrates: 62g** • **Fiber: 7g**
Protein: 14g

Pasta, Zucchini & Eggplant Salad
Serves 6-8

Ingredients
1 lb. brown rice fusilli
2 eggplant
2 zucchini
3 carrots
1 large red onion, cut into 1/2-inch slices
1 green pepper, chopped
1/4 cup grapeseed oil
1/2 tsp. Pink Himalayan sea salt
1/4 tsp. fresh cracked pepper
1 small package cherry tomatoes, halved
1 1/2 cups (6 oz.) crumbled feta cheese
2 Tbsp. fresh parsley, minced

Parmesan Vinaigrette
3/4 cup olive oil
1/3 cup grated Parmesan cheese
1/3 cup balsamic vinegar
3 Tbsp. lemon juice
1 tsp. honey

1 garlic clove, minced
1 tsp. sea salt
1/2 tsp. dried oregano
1/2 tsp. pepper

Directions

Cook pasta according to package directions; drain and rinse in cold water. Place in a large bowl and set aside.

Meanwhile, cut the eggplant, zucchini and carrots lengthwise into 3/4-inch-thick slices. Brush the eggplant, zucchini, carrots, onion and pepper with grapeseed oil; sprinkle with sea salt and pepper. Grill vegetables, covered, over medium heat for 4-6 minutes on each side or until tender, yet slightly crisp. When cool enough to touch, cut into cubes.

Add the tomatoes, feta cheese, parsley and grilled vegetables to the pasta. In a small bowl, whisk the vinaigrette ingredients. Pour over salad; toss to coat. Cover and refrigerate until serving.

NUTRITION
PER SERVING

Fats: 23g • Carbohydrates: 56g • Fiber: 6g
Protein: 34g

Phenom Chicken & Date Wraps
Serves 2-4

Ingredients
2-4 whole wheat or gluten-free wraps
1 chicken breast
8 dates, pitted & sliced
8 oz. small curd plain cottage cheese
2 Tbsp. grapeseed oil

Directions
Slice chicken breast into thin strips and cook in grapeseed oil and set aside.
Spread thin layer of cottage cheese on wraps and line with dates and chicken strips.
Wrap and eat!

NUTRITION PER SERVING | Fats: 20g • Carbohydrates: 47g • Fiber: 14g
Protein: 13g

Quinoa Southwest Salad
Serves 2-4

Ingredients
1 cup quinoa
1 can black beans (drained)
2 garlic cloves, minced
1/2 cup celery, chopped
1 carrot, diced
1 cup fresh green beans, chopped
1/2 cup red bell pepper, diced
1/2 cup green bell pepper, diced
1 medium vine-ripened tomato, sliced
1 cup cucumber, chopped
1/4 cup sliced olives
2 Tbsp. fresh basil, chopped
1/4 cup green onions, chopped
2 Tbsp. grapeseed oil
3 Tbsp. extra virgin olive oil (for dressing)

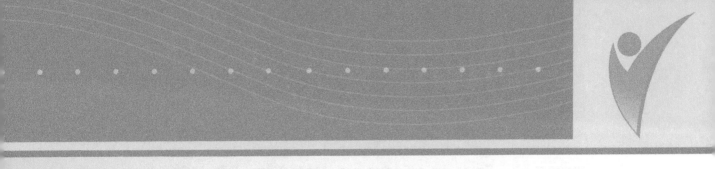

Directions

Cook quinoa according to package directions and set aside.

Together, sauté garlic, carrot, peppers, green beans and celery in 2 Tbsp. of grapeseed oil for about 5 minutes until soft.

Transfer quinoa and veggies to large bowl and mix.

Add in all additional ingredients and mix thoroughly.

Dish into individual serving bowls and drizzle with extra virgin olive oil.

Add sea salt and pepper to taste.

NUTRITION
PER SERVING | **Fats: 4g • Carbohydrates: 27g • Fiber: 8g**
Protein: 10g

Quinoa Veggie Bake
Serves 4-6

Ingredients
1 cup quinoa, cooked according to package directions & set aside
1 bunch of baby broccoli, chopped
1 cup carrots, finely diced
2 cloves garlic, minced
1 Tbsp. Vegenaise
1/2 cup nutritional yeast (or Parmesan cheese)
dash of sea salt, to taste
dash of pepper, to taste

Directions
Preheat oven to 350 degrees.
Combine cooked quinoa and rest of ingredients in casserole dish and top
with a few more sprinkles of nutritional yeast (or Parmesan cheese).
Bake 20 minutes.
Enjoy!

NUTRITION
PER SERVING | Fats: 12g • Carbohydrates: 23g • Fiber: 5g
Protein: 7g

Roasted Zucchini Flatbread
Serves 4

Ingredients
1 lb. or 4 small zucchini, cut into 1/2-inch thick rounds
2 Tbsp. grapeseed oil
dash of Pink Himalayan sea salt
4 round, whole-grain or gluten-free pita
1/3 cup of your favorite organic hummus
1/4 cup crumbled goat cheese
2 cups baby spinach

Directions
Preheat the oven to 400 degrees. Place the zucchini on a baking sheet.
Drizzle with the grapeseed oil, then sprinkle with 1 tsp. sea salt; mix well and
spread to 1 layer. Roast until browned and very tender, about 30 minutes,
stirring halfway through.
Lightly toast the pita on a grill or griddle until nicely toasted, but still soft,
and spread each with 1 heaping Tbsp. hummus. Top each piece with 1 Tbsp.
crumbled goat cheese, 1/4 of the roasted zucchini and about 1/2 cup baby
spinach. Serve warm.

GOAT CHEESE

Goat cheese has about half the cholesterol, fat and calories as regular cream cheese.
Try it as a substitute on gluten-free toast with lox (smoked salmon) instead of cream cheese.

NUTRITION PER SERVING | **Fats: 52g • Carbohydrates: 45g • Fiber: 6g
Protein: 25g**

Salmon & Greens Salad
Serves 1

Ingredients
4 oz. Wild Alaska Salmon (canned, water drained)
large handful baby spinach
1/4 cup black beans
2 Tbsp. extra virgin olive oil
1/4 cup raisins
(optional: add 1 or 2 hard-boiled eggs to the salad to beef it up)

Directions
In bowl, combine spinach, raisins and chickpeas.
In small pot, slowly warm the salmon and then add into salad.
Drizzle olive oil over top of salad. Enjoy!

NUTRITION
PER SERVING

**Fats: 11g • Carbohydrates: 39g • Fiber: 13g
Protein: 14g**

Santorini Island Salad
Serves 2-4

Ingredients
4 cups arugula & spinach mix
1/4 cup feta cheese crumbles
1 red onion, chopped
2 pieces of celery chopped
1 1/2 cups chickpeas
1/2 cup black pitted olives
1/2 cucumber, peeled & chopped

Directions
Put into large bowl and mix well. Top with Santorini Dressing (next recipe).

NUTRITION
PER SERVING | **Fats: 44g • Carbohydrates: 40g • Fiber: 9g**
Protein: 8g

Santorini Island Dressing
Serves 2

Ingredients
1 Tbsp. apple cider vinegar
3 sun-dried tomatoes, chopped
3 Tbsp. extra virgin olive oil
1 garlic clove, minced
1 lemon (juice & zest)
zest is grated lemon peel
salt & pepper to taste

Directions
Put ingredients in a bowl, whisk together until smooth and mix into salad.

NUTRITION PER SERVING | Fats: 1g • Carbohydrates: 36g • Fiber: 8g
Protein: 3g

Simple Spinach Salad
Serves 1

Note: This is a great weight-cutting meal when you need to be light but want to keep your energy high.

Ingredients
handful fresh spinach leaves
handful brightly colored vegetables of your choice, chopped
handful fruit, chopped

Dressing
light drizzle of hemp oil & apple cider vinegar

Directions
Mix all ingredients in bowl and top with dressing.

LUNCH

NUTRITION PER SERVING | **Fats: 39g • Carbohydrates: 16g • Fiber: 4g Protein: 67g**

Sirloin Steak Salad
Serves 4

Ingredients
1 3/4 lbs. grass-fed sirloin steak
1/3 cup grapeseed oil
3 Tbsp. red wine vinegar
2 Tbsp. lemon juice
1 clove garlic, minced
1/2 tsp. salt
1/8 tsp. ground black pepper
1 tsp. Dijon mustard
3/4 cup crumbled feta (or cheese of your choice)
8 cups baby spinach
2 tomatoes, sliced
1 small green bell pepper, sliced
1 carrot, sliced
1/2 cup sliced red onion
1/4 cup black olives (optional)

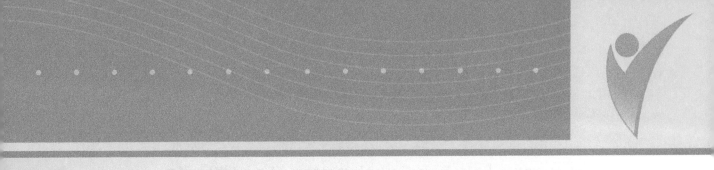

Directions

Place a pan on medium heat and lightly oil with grapeseed oil. Place steak on pan and cook for 3 to 5 minutes per side or until desired doneness is reached. Remove from heat and let sit until cool enough to handle. Slice steak into bite-sized pieces.

In a small bowl, whisk together the olive oil, vinegar, lemon juice, garlic, salt, pepper and Dijon mustard. Cover and place dressing in refrigerator.

Place spinach, tomato, pepper, carrot, onion and olives in large, individual salad bowls. Top with steak and feta cheese crumbles. Drizzle with dressing.

Enjoy!

NUTRITION **PER SERVING** | Fats: 8g • Carbohydrates: 35g • Fiber: 4g
Protein: 7g

Spinach, Pinto Bean & Potato Soup
Serves 4-6

Ingredients
2 Tbsp. grapeseed oil
1 onion, diced
1 stalk celery, chopped
2 carrots, peeled and diced
8 oz. red potatoes, cut into 1-inch pieces
Pink Himalayan sea salt and freshly ground pepper, to taste
5 cups torn baby spinach leaves
1 (15 oz.) can pinto beans, drained and rinsed
2 tsp. red-wine vinegar

Directions
Heat oil in a large pot over medium heat. Add onion, celery and carrots to
pot and sauté until tender, 6 to 8 minutes.
Add potatoes and 4 cups water. Add dash of sea salt and pepper, to taste.
Bring to a boil and then reduce to low. Let cook until potatoes are tender,
about 12 minutes. Mash half the contents of the pot until slightly thickened.
Add spinach and beans and continue cooking until spinach is tender, about 8
minutes. Stir in vinegar.

NUTRITION PER SERVING | Fats: 9g • Carbohydrates: 73g • Fiber: 15g
Protein: 24g

Spinach & Tomato Barley Bake
Serves 4-6

Ingredients
5 1/2 cups water
1 1/2 cups pearl barley
1/4 cup tomato paste
2 large cloves garlic
2 cups fresh spinach leaves
1 cup fresh basil leaves
2 dozen cherry tomatoes, halved
1 tsp. salt
black pepper, to taste
1 egg
1 cup low-fat cottage cheese
1 cup shredded mozzarella cheese

Directions
Bring water to a boil. Add barley and cook 35-40 minutes, or until most of
the water is absorbed and the barley is tender (taste it). Drain off any excess
water. Stir tomato paste into the barley and set aside.
Preheat the oven to 350 degrees. Wipe the inside of 9" by 13" baking dish
with grapeseed oil.

Finely chop the garlic, spinach and basil.

Add the chopped garlic, spinach, basil and tomatoes to the barley and stir. Add salt, pepper, egg and cottage cheese and mix well.

Spoon the barley mixture into the prepared dish and evenly distribute it throughout the dish. Bake 30 minutes. Sprinkle with mozzarella cheese. Bake another 10 minutes until cheese is melted and slightly browned. Serve and enjoy!

NUTRITION
PER SERVING | **Fats: 37g • Carbohydrates: 26g • Fiber: 13g**
Protein: 41g

Strawberry Salad
Serves 1

Ingredients
2 handfuls baby spinach
10 fresh strawberries, sliced
1/2 avocado, cut into bite-sized chunks
1 cup walnuts

Directions
Arrange spinach, avocado, walnuts and strawberries in bowl.
Dressing: light drizzle of extra virgin olive oil and balsamic vinegar

**Fats: 22g • Carbohydrates: 34g • Fiber: 13g
Protein: 37g**

Supafly Chicken Salad
Serves 2

Ingredients
8 oz. chicken breast, cut into bite-sized pieces
1/2 celery stalk, chopped
1 cup grapes, halved
1 cup chickpeas
1 avocado, peeled & pitted
1 tsp. lemon juice
sea salt & pepper, to taste

Directions
Lightly coat pan with grapeseed oil and cook chicken over low-medium heat.
Combine rest of ingredients in large bowl and mix well, mashing avocado into mixture.
Once chicken is cooked, let cool and then add to rest of ingredients in bowl and mix well.
Chill until serving.
This salad can be served a number of ways: on a bed of lettuce, on whole grain bread or in a gluten-free wrap.

NUTRITION
PER SERVING

**Fats: 11g • Carbohydrates: 9g • Fiber: 4g
Protein: 24g**

Tuna Salad
Serves 2

Ingredients
1 can tuna in water
1/4 onion, chopped
1/2 celery stalk, chopped
1/2 avocado
1-2 Tbsp. brown spicy mustard
1 Tbsp. sweet pickle relish
1 hard-boiled egg

Directions
Mix all ingredients together and put on whole wheat or gluten-free bread, in wrap or enjoy over green salad.

FOOD | FACTOIDS

TUNA FISH

The omega-3 content in tuna can help stave off dementia, depression and asthma.

NUTRITION
PER SERVING
| **Fats: 10g • Carbohydrates: 9g • Fiber: 1g**
Protein: 8g

Tuna-Stuffed Tomatoes
Serves 1-2

Ingredients
2 large vine-ripened tomatoes
1 can tuna in water, drained
2 Tbsp. Vegenaise
dash of sea salt
dash of black pepper

Directions
Wash and core tomatoes and set aside.
In a small bowl, combine tuna, Vegenaise, salt and pepper and mix well.
Stuff tuna mixture into tomatoes.
Enjoy!

Turkey & Cranberries Brown Rice Salad
Serves 2-4

Ingredients
2 cups turkey breast, cooked and cut into bite-sized pieces
2 cups cooked brown rice
1 cup red grapes, halved
1/2 cup dried cranberries
1/2 cup chopped pecans

Raspberry Vinaigrette
1/4 cup raspberry vinegar
1 1/2 Tbsp. honey
1 1/2 tsp. Dijon mustard
1/2 cup fresh or frozen organic red raspberries, crushed
1/2 cup organic extra virgin olive oil
dash of Pink Himalayan sea salt and ground pepper

Directions
Combine all ingredients in a large bowl.
In a small bowl, whisk the vinaigrette ingredients, except olive oil, then slowly add in olive oil, whisking until blended.
Drizzle with vinaigrette (or extra virgin olive oil and balsamic vinegar) and toss to coat.

NUTRITION
PER SERVING | **Fats: 1.5g • Carbohydrates: 40g • Fiber: 10g**
Protein: 8g

Vegan Veggie Soup
Makes 2 quarts

Ingredients
8 cups Organic Vegetable Broth (we've used Pacific Organics or Imagine brands)
1 oz. button mushrooms (or your favorite kind)
2 carrots, diced
2 stalks celery, diced
3 large red potatoes, diced
1 cup chickpeas, rinsed and drained
1 cup black beans, rinsed and drained
1 small bunch spinach (about 6 oz.)
1 tsp. Bragg's Liquid Aminos
pinch of sea salt and freshly ground black pepper
1 to 2 Tbsp. fresh lemon juice
2 Tbsp. chopped fresh parsley leaves

Directions
Add mushrooms, broth, carrots, celery, potatoes, chickpeas, beans, spinach and Bragg Liquid Aminos to a large pot. Bring to a boil over medium-high heat, reduce to a simmer, and cook, stirring occasionally, until potatoes are completely tender and beginning to fall apart, about 25 minutes. Season to taste with salt and pepper, stir in lemon juice and parsley, and serve.

NUTRITION PER SERVING | **Fats: 24g • Carbohydrates: 65g • Fiber: 13g
Protein: 15g**

Waldorf Salad
Serves 2-4

Ingredients
1/2 cup chopped walnuts
1/2 cup plain yogurt
2 Tbsp. avocado
2 Tbsp. parsley, minced
1 tsp. honey
freshly ground black pepper to taste
2 large apples, chopped into 1/2-inch pieces
2 celery stalks, chopped
1/4 cup raisins
1/2 lemon, juiced
1 head Romaine lettuce, shredded into bite-sized pieces

Directions
Mix yogurt, avocado, parsley, honey and pepper in a bowl. Add the apples, celery and raisins and sprinkle with the lemon juice; toss with yogurt mixture. Wait to add walnuts and lettuce until you're ready to eat the salad. Chill before serving.

NUTRITION PER SERVING | **Fat: 77g • Carbohydrates: 76g • Fiber: 13g**
Protein: 43g

Waldorf Turkey Sandwich

Ingredients
1 apple, thinly sliced
1 tablespoon Dijon mustard
1/4 cup chopped walnuts (optional)
1/3 cup Organic Vegenaise
2 slices of whole wheat or gluten-free bread
fresh, thinly sliced turkey
Handful fresh baby spinach

Directions
Mix mustard and walnuts with Vegenaise. Spread it on bread slices, then layer on sliced turkey and apple. Top with spinach and other bread slice. Cut in half. Enjoy!

LUNCH

NUTRITION PER SERVING | **Fats: 3g • Carbohydrates: 49g • Fiber: 8g Protein: 5g**

Warm Apple Quinoa
Serves 1-2

Ingredients
1/2 cup quinoa, cooked
1/4 cup unsweetened almond milk
1 apple, chopped
1/4 tsp. vanilla extract
dash of Saigon cinnamon

Directions
Mix ingredients in small pot and heat until warm. Serve and enjoy!

Warm Quinoa, Chickpea & Veggie Bowl
Serves 2-4

Ingredients
1 cup quinoa
1 Tbsp. grapeseed oil
1 red bell pepper
1 green bell pepper
3/4 cup chickpeas
about 14 cherry tomatoes
1/4 cup red onion, chopped

Directions
Cook quinoa according to package directions and set aside to cool.
Slice peppers and onions and sauté in grapeseed oil for a few minutes until soft.
Toss tomatoes into the pan with the peppers/onions mix. Sauté for another 2-3 minutes until tomato skin begin to crumple.
Now add in chickpeas and sauté another minute.
Time to serve! Scoop quinoa into individual serving bowls and then top with veggie mixture. Enjoy!

NUTRITION PER SERVING | Fats: 11g • Carbohydrates: 50g • Fiber: 12g
Protein: 16g

Zucchini, Black Bean & Quinoa Soup
Serves 4-6

Ingredients
6 cups low-sodium chicken broth
1 cup uncooked quinoa
1 large onion, sliced
1 1/2 cups black beans
2 large carrots, chopped
3 cloves garlic, minced
3 Tbsp. grapeseed oil
1 lb. zucchini, chopped
1 lb. kale leaves, chopped
dash of sea salt
dash of black pepper

Directions
In a large pot bring chicken broth to a boil and add in quinoa. Lower to a simmer and cover. Cook for about 30-40 minutes or until quinoa is soft.
Meanwhile, in large pan, sauté onions, carrots and garlic in grapeseed oil until tender.
Add in zucchini and cook about 5 minutes.
Mix in kale and cook until wilted, then set aside.

When quinoa is soft, stir in black beans along with veggie mixture.
Season with salt and pepper. The soup should be pretty thick. You can thin it out with additional broth if you'd like.
Enjoy!

NUTRITION PER SERVING	**Fats: 27g • Carbohydrates: 0g • Fiber: 0g** **Protein: 1g**

ADDITIONAL DRESSINGS

Grapeseed Pesto

Ingredients
1 1/2 cups fresh basil leaves
1/2 cup grapeseed oil

Directions
Grind basil to a fine paste with mortar and pestle* and put in small bowl.
Add grapeseed oil and stir.

*You can also use a blender or food processor.

Nature's Dressing

hemp oil, add to taste
apple cider vinegar, add to taste

NUTRITION PER SERVING | **Fats: 2.5g • Carbohydrates: 0g • Fiber: 0g Protein: 0g**

Oil & Vinegar Dressing

extra virgin olive oil, add to taste
balsamic vinegar, add to taste

Strawberry Vinaigrette

Ingredients
1/2 cup extra virgin olive oil
1/2 pint fresh strawberries, halved
2 Tbsp. balsamic vinegar
1/2 tsp. sea salt
1/4 tsp. black pepper

Directions
Blend all ingredients until smooth. Serve over salad.

DINNER

NUTRITION
PER SERVING | **Fats: 35g • Carbohydrates: 33g • Fiber: 7g**
Protein: 5g

Apple Pecan Salad
Serves 2-4

Ingredients
2 large handfuls baby spinach
2 handfuls arugula
1/2 cup alfalfa sprouts
1 apple, chopped
1/2 cup chickpeas
2 Tbsp. chopped pecans
2 Tbsp. dried cranberries

Dressing
4 Tbsp. extra virgin olive oil
2 Tbsp. apple cider vinegar
dash of black pepper

Directions
In a small bowl, whisk together apple cider vinegar and olive oil with a dash of black pepper.
In a large bowl, combine everything else.
Separate portions in serving bowls and drizzle with dressing.
Enjoy!

Baked Chicken Dinner
Serves 1-2

Ingredients
1 chicken breast, sliced in half lengthwise
dash of sea salt
dash of pepper

Directions
Preheat oven to 350 degrees.
Rub chicken with grapeseed oil and sprinkle with sea salt and pepper. Place in baking dish and cook for 20 minutes or until no longer pink inside.

NUTRITION PER SERVING | **Fats: 14g • Carbohydrates: 34g • Fiber: 0g Protein: 26g**

Baked Curry-Glazed Chicken
Serves 4

Ingredients
1/2 cup honey
1/4 cup butter, melted
1/4 cup yellow mustard
1 tsp. salt
1 tsp. curry powder
4 skinless boneless chicken breasts

Directions
Heat oven to 375 degrees. Stir together first 5 ingredients in a shallow dish until blended. Dip chicken in honey mixture, 1 piece at a time, thoroughly coating all sides. Arrange chicken, skin side up, in a single layer in a casserole dish. Then pour remaining honey mixture over chicken.
Bake for 40-45 minutes.

FOOD | FACTOIDS

HONEY

A spoonful of honey before a workout can help keep you going a little bit longer. The glucose from honey provides immediate energy since it is absorbed so quickly, while the fructose is reserved for sustained energy. Just think—an extra spoonful for that extra mile!

NUTRITION PER SERVING | Fats: 60g • Carbohydrates: 77g • Fiber: 12g
Protein: 69g

Buckwheat Chicken Parmesan
Serves 2-4

Ingredients
2 chicken breasts, sliced thin
2 eggs
1/4 cup almond milk
1 cup buckwheat
1 can diced tomatoes
4 Tbsp. grapeseed oil
1 1/2 cup fresh mozzarella shredded*
*can substitute veggie cheese or nutritional yeast

Directions
Preheat oven to 350 degrees.
Add grapeseed oil to large pan and put on low to medium heat.
Combine eggs and almond milk in small bowl and whisk together well.
Put buckwheat in a separate small bowl.
Dip each piece of chicken (one at a time) first in the egg mixture and then in the buckwheat flakes and place into pan.
Cook the chicken on both sides until tender and outsides are slightly browned.

Place chicken in 9 x 12 casserole dish and cover with diced tomatoes and their juices.

Cover with aluminum foil and bake 30 minutes. Remove from oven, top with fresh mozzarella and put back in oven, uncovered, for about 10 minutes or until cheese is melted and slightly browned.

NUTRITION | Fats: 56g • Carbohydrates: 96g • Fiber: 19g
PER SERVING | Protein: 44g

Buckwheat Eggplant Parmesan
Serves 2-4

Ingredients
1 large eggplant, peeled & cut into 1/4-inch round slices
2 eggs (Vegan option = use egg replacement)
1/4 cup almond milk
1 cup buckwheat
1 can diced tomatoes
4 Tbsp. grapeseed oil
1 1/2 cups fresh mozzarella, shredded (Vegan = can substitute veggie cheese or nutritional yeast)

Directions
Preheat oven to 350 degrees.
Add grapeseed oil to large pan and put on low to medium heat.
Combine eggs and almond milk in small bowl and whisk together well.
Put buckwheat in a separate small bowl.
Dip each piece of eggplant (one at a time) first in the egg mixture and then in the buckwheat flakes and place into pan.
Cook the eggplant on both sides until tender and outsides are slightly browned.

Place eggplant in 9 x 12 casserole dish and cover with diced tomatoes and their juices.
Cover with aluminum foil and bake 30 minutes. Remove from oven, top with fresh mozzarella and put back in oven, uncovered, for about 10 minutes or until cheese is melted and slightly browned.

NUTRITION PER SERVING | **Fats: 17g • Carbohydrates: 40g • Fiber: 10g**
Protein: 32g

Champion Chili
Serves 4-6

Ingredients
1/2 lb. ground organic turkey - or 1 can chickpeas
2 cans diced tomatoes or 6-7 freshly chopped tomatoes
1 can kidney beans
1 red pepper, chopped
1 green pepper, chopped
1 sweet onion, chopped
4 cloves garlic, chopped
sea salt, to taste
chili powder, to taste
1 cup shredded rice cheddar cheese (optional)

Directions
Put tomatoes and beans in large pot and place on low heat.
Brown meat in separate pan and add to tomato pot.
In another pan, sauté peppers, onions and garlic in grapeseed oil. Once tender, add to tomato pot.
Add sea salt and chili powder to taste.
Sprinkle with cheese and serve.

NUTRITION | **Fats: 5g • Carbohydrates: 22g • Fiber: 6g**
PER SERVING | **Protein: 36g**

Chicken & Asparagus Stir-Fry
Serves 2-4

Ingredients
2 chicken breasts cut into bite-sized pieces
1 bunch thin asparagus (about 20 stalks)
2 cloves garlic, chopped
1 medium shallot, minced
2 Tbsp. Bragg Liquid Aminos or low-sodium soy sauce or teriyaki sauce

Directions
Cut off thick ends of asparagus; wash what remains and cut into bite-sized pieces.
Steam for about 7-10 minutes, or until bright green, and then set aside.
In a large pan, sauté shallot and garlic in peanut oil for about 2 minutes.
Add chicken and continue to sauté about 6 minutes or until pink disappears.
Pour into heat-safe serving bowl and mix in asparagus.
Add 2 Tbsp. Bragg Liquid Aminos or low-sodium soy sauce/ teriyaki sauce and serve.

FOOD | FACTOIDS

ASPARAGUS

Asparagus is a rich source of glutathione, a compound that helps break down carcinogens and free radicals, which makes it a great cancer-fighting food.

NUTRITION PER SERVING	**Fats: 71g • Carbohydrates: 98g • Fiber: 23g** **Protein: 61g**

The Chicken Burger
Serves 2-4

1 lb. ground chicken
1 shallot, diced
1 Tbsp. garlic, minced
1/2 cup crimini mushrooms
1 egg
4 Tbsp. grapeseed oil
1 green bell pepper, chopped
4 whole wheat or gluten-free buns (or go Protein style & wrap in butter lettuce leaves!)
large handful baby spinach leaves
1 large avocado, sliced
1 large vine-ripened tomato, sliced
1/2 cup oat bran (or buckwheat for gluten-free option)
1 tsp. sea salt
1 Tbsp. black pepper

Directions
In large pan, add 2 Tbsp. grapeseed oil and sauté the shallot, bell pepper and garlic until tender.

Add in the mushrooms and stir for about 2 minutes or until mushrooms brown. Set aside and let vegetables cool.

Next, in a large bowl, combine the chicken, vegetables, egg, oat bran, salt and pepper.

Mix all ingredients together and form into 8 patties.

Heat 2 Tbsp. grapeseed oil in large pan and cook each chicken patty over medium heat for about 5 minutes on each side until cooked through.

Place burger on buns or lettuce leaves and top with tomato, avocado and spinach. Add ketchup or mustard to taste. Enjoy!

NUTRITION PER SERVING | **Fats: 28g • Carbohydrates: 74g • Fiber: 6g**
Protein: 45g

Chicken & Egg Noodles
Serves 4

Ingredients
2 Tbsp. grapeseed oil
3/4 lb. boneless, skinless chicken breast, cut into bite-sized pieces
1/3 cup onion, finely chopped
1 can (14 oz.) organic chicken broth (we like Pacific or Imagine brands)
1/2 package (12 oz.) egg noodles (we like No-Yolk Egg Noodles, Broad)
1 package (10 oz.) organic fresh peas and carrots, chopped (frozen is ok, too)
1 package (10 oz.) organic cream of chicken or cream of mushroom soup (we like Pacific or Imagine brands)
3/4 cup almond milk
3/4 cup Parmesan cheese, grated

Directions
Heat grapeseed oil in large pan over medium heat, add chicken and stir to heat all sides of the pieces. Add onion; continue to mix. Cook 5 minutes or until chicken is no longer pink. Add chicken broth; heat to boiling. Stir in uncooked pasta and peas and carrots, stirring to coat evenly with liquid. Heat to boiling; reduce heat. Cover; simmer on medium heat 10 minutes, stirring occasionally, until most liquid is absorbed. Meanwhile, in a medium bowl, stir together soup, almond milk and about a 1/2 cup Parmesan cheese until smooth. Stir into pasta mixture. Simmer until heated through. Serve sprinkled with remaining cheese.

NUTRITION PER SERVING | **Fats: 21g • Carbohydrates: 38g • Fiber: 8g
Protein: 37g**

Chicken Asparagus Protein Skillet
Serves 2-4

Ingredients
1 Tbsp. grapeseed oil
2 peeled garlic cloves, plus 1/2 tsp. minced garlic
1 cups whole wheat or gluten free bread crumbs
dash of Pink Himalayan sea salt
dash of freshly ground black pepper
1 1/2 lbs. thin asparagus, cut in 1- to 2-inch lengths
1 bunch green onions, chopped
8 large eggs, beaten
1/2 tsp. paprika
2 Tbsp. parsley, chopped
2 skinless boneless chicken breasts, chopped into bite-sized pieces

Directions
Put 1 Tbsp. grapeseed oil in a large pan over medium heat. Add peeled garlic cloves and let them sizzle until lightly browned, then remove. Add bread crumbs, season with salt and pepper, lower heat to medium and gently cook until lightly browned and crisp, about 2 minutes. Remove bread and set aside to cool.

In a separate pan, heat 1 Tbsp. grapeseed oil and add chopped chicken. Cook through and set aside.
Meanwhile, add asparagus to first pan and cook until tender, about 4 minutes. Add green onions and minced garlic and cook 1 minute more.

Season eggs with salt, pepper and paprika. Pour into pan and cook, mixing often until eggs firm up, for about 3 minutes. Add in chicken and gently stir. Add parsley and serve immediately, topped with the bread cubes.
Enjoy!

DINNER

NUTRITION
PER SERVING | **Fats: 6g • Carbohydrates: 4g • Fiber: 0g**
Protein: 29g

Cider-Glazed Chicken
Serves 4

Ingredients
1 tsp. grass-fed butter
4 skinless boneless chicken breasts
3/4 tsp. Pink Himalayan sea salt, divided
1/4 tsp. freshly ground black pepper
1/2 cup apple cider
1 tsp. Dijon mustard

Directions
Melt 1 tsp. grass-fed butter in a large pan over medium heat. Sprinkle chicken with salt and pepper. Add chicken to pan; cook 3 minutes on each side or until done. Remove from pan. Add cider and mustard to pan, scraping pan to loosen browned bits; cook 2 to 3 minutes or until syrupy. Add chicken to pan, turning to coat. Remove from heat. Serve and enjoy!

DINNER

NUTRITION
PER SERVING

**Fats: 35g • Carbohydrates: 28g • Fiber: 5g
Protein: 32g**

Cinnamon Orange Pecan Chicken
Serves 4-6

Ingredients
4 skinless, boneless chicken breasts, each sliced in half lengthwise
4 Tbsp. organic maple syrup
1 cup pecans, crushed
3 Tbsp. grapeseed oil
dash of sea salt
dash of black pepper
3 oranges, 2 sliced into wedges & 1 juiced (if you don't own a juicer, just squeeze it!)
1 tsp. ground cumin
1/2 tsp. cayenne pepper
1 Tbsp. cinnamon

Directions
Trim any fatty parts from chicken breasts.
Place maple syrup in bowl and crushed pecans in another.
Roll chicken in 2 Tbsp. maple syrup and then in the crushed pecans.
Drizzle 3 Tbsp. grapeseed oil in pan and turn on medium heat.
Sprinkle chicken with salt and pepper and place in pan.

Drizzle with 1 Tbsp. syrup and press the rest of the pecans from the bowl onto the chicken breasts.
Cook about 4 minutes on each side until cooked through.

In a small pan, add orange juice, 1 Tbsp. syrup, cayenne and cumin.
Cook uncovered about 1-2 minutes until thickened.
Put chicken on serving plates and pour orange mixture over chicken.
Sprinkle with a pinch of cinnamon and serve with orange wedges.

NUTRITION
PER SERVING

Fats: 8g • Carbohydrates: 88g • Fiber: 23g
Protein: 36g

Classic Red Beans & Rice (With Chicken)
Serves 4-6

Ingredients
2 chicken breasts, thinly sliced - or leave out (Vegan option)
1 yellow onion, diced
1 stalk celery, chopped
1 green pepper, diced
1 garlic clove, minced
1 Tbsp. grapeseed oil
3 (15-oz.) cans red beans, rinsed & drained
Note: Red beans & kidney beans are not the same, although one can be substituted for the other.
1 (16-oz.) can tomato paste
1 (14 1/2-oz.) can diced tomatoes
1 1/2 cups water
1/4 tsp. oregano
1/4 tsp. thyme
1/4 tsp. sage
1 Tbsp. parsley
dash of sea salt
dash of black pepper

1/4 tsp. Tabasco (optional)
1 bay leaf
1 cup brown rice, cooked according to package directions

Directions

Cook the chicken breast slices in one pan with grapeseed oil and set aside.

In another pan, cook the green pepper, celery, onion and garlic until vegetables are soft.

Now add the beans, tomato paste, tomatoes (with juice), water, all the spices, Tabasco and bay leaf.

Cook 10 minutes, stirring often. Reduce to a simmer, mix in chicken and cook another 10 minutes.

Remove bay leaf. Serve over rice (or quinoa). Enjoy!

NUTRITION PER SERVING | **Fats: 56g • Carbohydrates: 20g • Fiber: 4g**
Protein: 45g

Coconut Tropical Chicken
Serves 2-4

Ingredients
2 chicken breasts, sliced in half lengthwise
2 eggs
1/4 cup almond milk
1/4 cup oat bran - or buckwheat
1/4 cup ground flax seed
1/4 cup unsweetened coconut flakes
4 Tbsp. unrefined coconut oil

Directions
Combine eggs and milk in one small bowl.
Combine flaxseed, coconut and oat bran in another small bowl.
Coat chicken first in the egg mixture and then roll it in the coconut mixture.
Place chicken pieces in large pan with coconut oil and cook on low to medium heat about 8-10 minutes, carefully flipping pieces once they start to brown.
Keeping the pan uncovered will allow coating to become crisp. For a softer coating, keep covered.
Once chicken is cooked through, serve with your favorite green veggies and enjoy!

DINNER

NUTRITION | Fats: 2g • Carbohydrates: 3g • Fiber: 1g
PER SERVING | Protein: 41g

Cod or Tilapia
Serves 1

Ingredients
1 cod or tilapia filet
1 dash each of sea salt, rosemary & pepper
1/2 lemon, juiced

Directions
Heat oven to 350 degrees.
Rub fish with grapeseed oil and spices.
Bake in casserole dish for 15 minutes.
Squeeze fresh lemon juice over filet and serve.

NUTRITION
PER SERVING | Fats: 17g • Carbohydrates: 38g • Fiber: 5g
Protein: 40g

Cream of Chicken Casserole With Jasmine Rice
Serves 6

Note: You can add vegetables of your choice to this!

Ingredients
1 (12 oz.) package Organic Condensed Cream of Chicken Soup (we used Pacific brand)
1 cup almond milk
1 cup dry organic jasmine brown rice, precooked
3 carrots, chopped
1 head broccoli, chopped
1 cup shredded organic cheddar cheese
6 (4 oz.) skinless, boneless chicken breast halves
dash of paprika
1 tsp. Pink Himalayan sea salt
dash of fresh ground pepper

Directions

Stir the soup, almond milk, precooked rice, vegetables and half the cheese in a casserole dish. Top with the chicken. Sprinkle the chicken with paprika, salt and pepper. Cover the baking dish.

Bake at 375 degrees for 50 minutes or until the chicken is cooked through. Veggies should be tender. Uncover the dish and sprinkle with the remaining cheese. Cook for another 10 minutes or until cheese on top is melted.

NUTRITION
PER SERVING | Fats: 8g • Carbohydrates: 32g • Fiber: 4g
Protein: 28g

Creamy Chicken Quinoa & Broccoli Casserole
Serves 6

Ingredients
2 cups organic free-range chicken broth (we like Pacific or Imagine brands)
1 cup almond milk
1 tsp. paprika
1/2 cup brown rice flour
2 cups water, divided
1 cup uncooked quinoa, rinsed
1/4 cup cooked, crumbled turkey bacon
1 lb. boneless skinless chicken breasts
2 tsp. Bragg Organic Sprinkle seasoning
1/4 cup shredded Swiss cheese
3 cups fresh broccoli florets

Directions
Sauce: Preheat the oven to 400 degrees and grease a 9" by 13" baking dish with grapeseed oil. Bring the chicken broth and 1/2 cup almond milk to a boil in a small pot. Whisk the other 1/2 cup almond milk with the paprika and flour; add the mixture to the broth mixture and whisk until smooth.
In a large bowl, mix the sauce, 1 cup water, quinoa and bacon, and stir to combine. Pour the mixture into the prepared baking dish. Slice the chicken

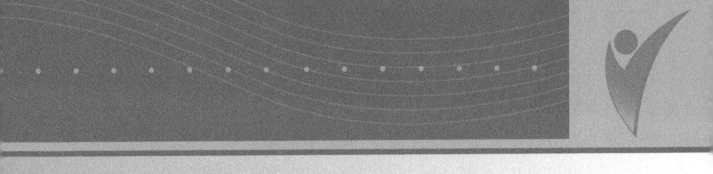

breasts into thin strips and lay the chicken breast strips over the top of the quinoa mixture. Sprinkle with the seasoning. Bake uncovered for 40-45 minutes.

While the casserole is in the oven, place the broccoli in boiling water for 1 minute until it turns bright green and then run under cold water. Set aside.

Alternatively, you can sauté the florets in a pan with some grapeseed oil until tender.

Next, remove the baking dish from the oven and check the consistency of the casserole. When the quinoa and chicken are cooked and the sauce is thickened, add the broccoli and a little bit of water until the consistency is creamy. Top with the Swiss cheese and bake for 5 minutes to melt the cheese.

Once chicken is cooked through, serve with your favorite green veggies and enjoy!

NUTRITION
PER SERVING | **Fats: 14g • Carbohydrates: 41g • Fiber: 6g
Protein: 9g**

Dates & Cashew Quinoa Salad
Serves 2

Ingredients
2-3 large handfuls baby spinach
1/2 cup cooked quinoa
1/2 cup whole cashews, crushed
1/2 cup dates, pitted & minced
sprinkle of feta cheese crumbles (optional)

Directions
Combine all ingredients except feta in large bowl and mix.
Divide salad into two bowls.
Add optional Honey Vinaigrette Dressing (next page) and sprinkle with feta.

FOOD | FACTOIDS

QUINOA

Quinoa is a perfect protein! It's considered a complete protein, which means it contains all of the essential amino acids. Just half a cup of quinoa has 14 grams of protein per serving and 6 grams of fiber! Plus, it's a whole grain AND gluten-free!

NUTRITION PER SERVING | Fats: 28g • Carbohydrates: 18g • Fiber: 0g
Protein: 0g

Honey Vinaigrette
Serves 2

Ingredients
2 Tbsp. honey
4 Tbsp. extra virgin olive oil
1 Tbsp. apple cider vinegar
1 Tbsp. water

Directions
Whisk honey, olive oil, vinegar and water in bowl until well combined and drizzle over salads.

NUTRITION PER SERVING | Fats: 12g • Carbohydrates: 35g • Fiber: 4g
Protein: 35g

Easy Lemon Chicken Potato Casserole
Serves 6-8

Ingredients
2 1/2 cups organic low-sodium condensed cream of mushroom or cream of chicken soup
1/2 cup almond milk
1 1/2 lbs. Yukon gold potatoes, very thinly sliced
2 cloves garlic, minced
1 small white onion, peeled and thinly sliced
1 1/2 lbs. boneless, skinless chicken breasts
dash of Pink Himalayan sea salt and freshly ground black pepper
1 lemon, thinly sliced and halved
(optional garnish: chopped fresh parsley or fresh thyme)

Directions
Preheat oven to 425 degrees.

Add soup and almond milk to a saucepan and whisk to combine. Heat over medium-high heat until simmering, stirring frequently. When it reaches a simmer, remove from heat and set aside.

In a separate large mixing bowl, add potatoes, onion, garlic and chicken. Pour in the soup mixture, along with a dash of sea salt and pepper, and gently toss to combine until the potato and chicken mixture is evenly coated.

Transfer mixture to a casserole dish. Add in lemon wedges. Then cover the top of dish with aluminum foil.

Bake for 1 hour or until the potatoes are tender. Change oven setting to broil and remove foil. Broil the casserole for an extra 2-3 minutes to crisp up the top. Remove pan from oven and serve warm.

DINNER

NUTRITION PER SERVING | **Fats: 34g • Carbohydrates: 70g • Fiber: 13g Protein: 18g**

The Emperor's New Salad
Serves 2-4

Ingredients
1/2 cup black rice
1 1/4 cups low-sodium chicken broth
1 onion, diced
2 cloves garlic, chopped
8 oz. crimini mushrooms, sliced
1 lb. baby broccoli, chopped
handful dill, chopped
3 Tbsp. grapeseed oil (for use in sautéing)
1/4 cup grapeseed oil
2-3 Tbsp. apple cider vinegar, to taste
4 cups arugula & baby spinach, mixed
1/4 cup feta, crumbled
sea salt, to taste
pepper, to taste

Directions
Preheat oven to 400 degrees.
Bring the broth to a boil and add black rice. Reduce the heat and simmer covered, until the rice is tender, about 50 minutes.

In about 20 minutes, after rice is cooking, heat 2 Tbsp. grapeseed oil in pan and begin sautéing onion and garlic about 3-5 minutes. Add in mushrooms and sauté about 5 minutes until mushrooms are browned. Season with salt and pepper to taste and set aside.

While onion mixture is cooking, toss broccoli in a bowl with the rest of the grapeseed oil.

Spread the broccoli out on a baking dish and roast in oven until tender, about 10-15 minutes.

Mix the black rice, dill, and onion mixture, olive oil and apple cider vinegar.

Serve with black rice on a bed of spinach and arugula mix, topped with roasted broccoli and sprinkles of crumbled feta.

NUTRITION
PER SERVING

Fats: 14g • Carbohydrates: 26g • Fiber: 4g
Protein: 11g

Farmer's Market Vegetarian Quesadillas
Serves 6

Ingredients
1/2 cup red bell pepper, chopped
1/2 cup zucchini, chopped
1/2 cup yellow squash, chopped
1/2 cup red onion, chopped
1/2 cup button mushrooms, chopped
1 Tbsp. grapeseed oil
6 (9 inch) whole wheat tortillas
1 1/4 cups shredded sharp cheddar cheese

Directions
Heat grapeseed oil in a large pan over medium heat. Add in red pepper, zucchini, yellow squash, onion and mushrooms. Cook for about 6-7 minutes, or until tender. Remove vegetables from pan.

Place one tortilla in pan. Sprinkle some of the cheese and vegetables onto the tortilla. Top with a second tortilla. Cook until golden on both sides, for approximately 2-3 minutes per side. Remove quesadilla from pan, and repeat with remaining ingredients. Cut each quesadilla into 8 triangles with a pizza cutter. Serve hot.

NUTRITION PER SERVING | **Fats: 20g • Carbohydrates: 69g • Fiber: 17g**
Protein: 45g

Fighter Fajitas
Serves 4-6

Ingredients
1 lb. skinless, boneless chicken breasts
16 oz. black beans
1 tsp. chili powder
1/2 tsp. sea salt
1/2 tsp. ground cumin
1/2 tsp. freshly ground black pepper
8-12 whole wheat or gluten-free tortillas

Toppings
1 avocado, mashed in bowl with 1 Tbsp. lemon juice. Set aside.
1 chopped tomato
1/4 head of lettuce, chopped
shredded cheddar cheese (optional)

Directions
Preheat oven to 350 degrees.
Coat pan in grapeseed oil and set on low-medium heat.
Combine chili powder, sea salt, cumin and black pepper in a small bowl.

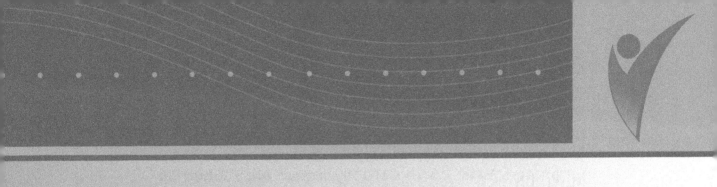

Chop raw chicken in bite-sized pieces and sprinkle with spices.
Place chicken in pan and cook 10 minutes, stirring often, until done.
Heat tortillas on cookie sheet in oven for 2 minutes and remove.
Divide chicken evenly among tortillas; top each tortilla with a sprinkle of lettuce, tomato, avocado and cheese.

NUTRITION
PER SERVING

Fats: 2.5g • Carbohydrates: 14g • Fiber: 5g
Protein: 20g

Garlic Portabella Chicken With Asparagus & Spinach
Serves 1-2

Ingredients
1/2 chicken breast, cut into bite-sized pieces – or eliminate chicken & use whole Portabella mushroom top (vegan option)
1/3 Portabella mushroom, chopped
handful baby spinach
1 Tbsp. garlic, minced
half bunch asparagus (6-8 stalks), steamed
dash each of sea salt, oregano & pepper

Directions
Coat medium pan with grapeseed oil and put on low-medium heat.
Add Portabella mushroom and garlic to pan.
Once mushrooms brown, add handful of spinach leaves and sauté until spinach shrinks into mushroom mixture.
Add asparagus.
In separate pan, sprinkle chicken with spices and sauté in grapeseed oil.
Once cooked, add chicken to mushroom pan. Lightly stir mixture.
Let cook together for 5 minutes, then plate.

NUTRITION
PER SERVING | Fats: 10g • Carbohydrates: 31g • Fiber: 5g
Protein: 7g

Ginger Veggie Stir-Fry
Serves 6

Ingredients
1 Tbsp. brown rice flour
1 1/2 cloves garlic, crushed
2 tsp. fresh ginger, chopped
4 Tbsp. grapeseed oil, divided
1 small head broccoli, cut into florets
1/2 cup snow peas
3/4 cup thinly sliced carrots
1/2 cup halved green beans
2 Tbsp. Bragg Liquid Aminos
2 1/2 Tbsp. water
1/4 cup chopped onion
1/2 Tbsp. Pink Himalayan sea salt
2 cups organic brown rice, cooked according to package directions

Directions
In a large bowl, blend brown rice flour, garlic, 1 tsp. ginger and 2 Tbsp. grape-seed oil until flour is dissolved. Mix in broccoli, snow peas, carrots and green beans, tossing to lightly coat.

Heat remaining 2 Tbsp. oil in a large pan over medium heat. Cook vegetables in oil for 3 minutes, stirring constantly to prevent burning. Stir in Bragg Liquid Aminos and water. Mix in onion, Pink Himalayan sea salt and remaining 1 tsp. ginger. Cook until vegetables are tender but still crisp. Serve over a bed of your favorite organic brown rice.

NUTRITION PER SERVING | Fats: 12g • Carbohydrates: 17g • Fiber: 0g
Protein: 56g

Honey-Glazed Salmon
Serves 1

Ingredients
8 oz. wild-caught salmon
dash of sea salt
1 Tbsp. honey or agave

Directions
Coat small pan with grapeseed oil and put on low-medium heat.
Rub salmon with grapeseed oil and sprinkle with sea salt.
Cook 3-5 minutes on each side, depending on thickness.
Salmon should be cooked evenly through the center.
Plate and drizzle with honey or agave.

NUTRITION
PER SERVING | Fats: 11g • Carbohydrates: 20g • Fiber: 6g
Protein: 6g

Layered Eggplant, Zucchini & Tomato Casserole
Serves 6

Ingredients
3 Tbsp. grapeseed oil
3 medium zucchini (1 1/2 lbs.), sliced lengthwise 1/3 inch thick
2 long, narrow eggplants (1 1/2 lbs.), peeled and sliced lengthwise 1/3 inch thick
dash of Pink Himalayan sea salt
dash of freshly ground pepper
1 large shallot, minced
1 lb. Roma tomatoes, diced
3 oz. feta cheese, crumbled (3/4 cup)
1/4 cup chopped basil
1/3 cup organic panko

Directions
Preheat the oven to 425 degrees. Brush 2 baking sheets with grapeseed oil. Put the zucchini slices on one sheet and the eggplant on the other. Brush the

slices all over with grapeseed oil and season with salt and pepper. Bake for 15 minutes or until tender.

Next, heat 2 Tbsp. of grapeseed oil in a large pan. Add the shallot and cook over medium heat a few minutes until softened. Add the tomatoes and cook over high heat until slightly softened and bubbling, 1 minute. Season with salt and pepper.

Next, in a casserole dish, place half of the eggplant in the dish and spread one-fourth of the tomatoes on top. Sprinkle on half of the feta and basil. Next, layer half of the zucchini on top, followed by another one-fourth of the tomato and the remaining basil, eggplant and zucchini. Top with the remaining tomato and feta. Mix the panko with the remaining 1 Tbsp. of oil and sprinkle over the casserole. Bake in the upper third of the oven for 20 minutes, until bubbling and

NUTRITION
PER SERVING

Fats: 23g • Carbohydrates: 73g • Fiber: 3g
Protein: 14g

Linguine With Tomatoes, Baby Zucchini & Herbs
Serves 4

Ingredients
1 lb. tomatoes, chopped
1 Tbsp. fresh basil, chopped
2 garlic cloves, minced
2 tsp. Pink Himalayan sea salt
1/3 cup extra-virgin olive oil
12 oz. linguine
3 baby zucchini, thinly sliced
1/4 cup freshly grated Parmesan cheese, plus more for serving

Directions
In a large bowl, toss the tomatoes with the basil, garlic, salt and olive oil. In a large pot of boiling salted water, cook the linguine until al dente (soft, yet slightly firm); drain well. Add the linguine to the bowl along with the sliced zucchini and toss. Add the 1/4 cup of grated cheese, toss again and serve in bowls.

| **NUTRITION** PER SERVING | Fats: 5g • Carbohydrates: 17g • Fiber: 1g Protein: 29g |

Marinated Chicken Teriyaki
Serves 2-4

Ingredients
4 boneless, skinless chicken breasts
1/2 fresh crushed pineapple (or one 8 oz. can)
2 Tbsp. Bragg Liquid Aminos
2 Tbsp. honey or agave
1 tsp. grated fresh ginger
1 small garlic clove, finely minced

Directions
Teriyaki Sauce: Place the crushed pineapple, Bragg Liquid Aminos, honey, ginger and garlic in a bowl; whisk to combine. Pour half of the teriyaki sauce in a resealable plastic bag and save the other half for later. Place the chicken breasts in the bag with the teriyaki sauce. Refrigerate for 30 minutes or up to overnight.

Turn on the broiler. Make sure the rack is in place in the center position. Place the marinated chicken breasts on a baking sheet or in a glass dish and add some of the marinade from the bag to the chicken. Broil for 8-10 minutes on each side.

Now heat the reserved teriyaki sauce in a small pot. Bring to a simmer and cook for 3 minutes or until thickened slightly.

When chicken is done, pour the teriyaki sauce over top and serve immediately.

DINNER

NUTRITION
PER SERVING | Fats: 5g • Carbohydrates: 86g • Fiber: 17g
Protein: 22g

Meatless Meatballs
Serves 4-6

Ingredients
16 oz. spaghetti (use your favorite kind). Cook & set aside.
For the meatballs:
1 small onion, chopped
5 oz. crimini mushrooms, chopped (optional)
1 tsp. black pepper
1/4 tsp. salt
1 (15-oz.) cans black beans, drained
3 garlic cloves, chopped
2 Tbsp. Worcestershire sauce (Vegan = use soy sauce or Bragg Liquid Aminos)
1/2 cup fresh parsley, chopped
1 cup oat bran (or buckwheat)
1/4 cup grated Parmesan or nutritional yeast

Directions
Preheat oven to 375 degrees and prepare a nonstick baking sheet by placing a piece of aluminum foil on it. Spread a thin layer of grapeseed oil over the foil with a paper towel.

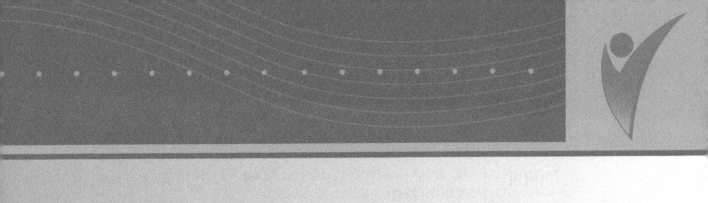

Combine all ingredients in a blender or food processor and mix until a thick batter forms.

Form 2-inch meatballs with your hands and place on baking sheet. Bake for about 12 minutes, then flip the meatballs and bake another 10 minutes.

Add the meatballs to your favorite pasta and sauce!

(Hint: These go great with the Power Pasta recipe!)

Enjoy!

NUTRITION
PER SERVING | **Fats: 20g • Carbohydrates: 23g • Fiber: 3g
Protein: 37g**

Mom's Meatloaf In A Pinch
Serves 4-6

Ingredients
1 lb. ground turkey
2 eggs
1 small onion, minced
2 garlic cloves, minced
1/2 cup oat bran (or buckwheat)
2 Tbsp. maple syrup
1 Tbsp. Worcestershire sauce
dash of sea salt
1 Tbsp. grapeseed oil

Directions
Preheat oven to 350 degrees.
In a large bowl, combine all ingredients and mix well.
Wipe grapeseed oil on inside of loaf pan and transfer mixture to the pan.
Bake for 45 minutes.
Remove from oven, slice and serve with your favorite sides.

FOOD | FACTOIDS

OATS

A cup of oat bran supplies 31% of an adult's daily requirement of selenium, which binds to protein to combat free radicals. Oat bran in itself is also an excellent source of protein.

NUTRITION PER SERVING | **Fats: 11g • Carbohydrates: 91g • Fiber: 11g**
Protein: 42g

Noodles A La Dolce
Serves 2-4

Ingredients
16 oz. of your favorite whole wheat or gluten-free pasta noodle
16 oz. plain 2% cottage cheese - or blend silken tofu with a dash of lemon juice
1/2 lb. ground turkey (optional)
sea salt, to taste
black pepper, to taste
1/4 cup nutritional yeast or Parmesan

Directions
Preheat oven to 350 degrees.
Boil noodles until soft, rinse and drain and add to a large casserole dish.
If using turkey meat, brown in pan and drain juices. Add to casserole dish.
Add cottage cheese to casserole dish along with salt and pepper. Mix well.
Sprinkle top of casserole with nutritional yeast or Parmesan and bake for 20-30 minutes until the tips of the noodles at the top of the casserole brown.
Serve and enjoy!

NUTRITION
PER SERVING

Fats: 5g • Carbohydrates: 23g • Fiber: 2g
Protein: 30g

Peach-Glazed Turkey Breast
Serves 4-6

Ingredients
4 boneless, skinless turkey breasts, each sliced in half lengthwise
3-4 peaches, sliced
2 Tbsp. agave
2 cloves garlic, minced
dash of sea salt
dash of black pepper

Directions
Preheat oven to 350 degrees.
Using small pan, sauté minced garlic in grapeseed oil for about 2 minutes and set aside.
Place turkey breasts in baking dish and place peach halves around them.
Drizzle turkey with agave and sprinkle with sautéed garlic, sea salt and pepper.
Bake about 45 minutes until turkey is done throughout.

NUTRITION
PER SERVING | Fats: 17g • Carbohydrates: 54g • Fiber: 8g
Protein: 16g

Penne Rigate With Brussels Sprouts & Gorgonzola
Serves 4

Ingredients
2 Tbsp. grapeseed oil
1 small red onion, thinly sliced
1 lb. Brussels sprouts, thinly sliced
1 tsp. chopped thyme
dash of Pink Himalayan sea salt
dash of freshly ground pepper
1/2 lb. penne rigate
4 oz. Gorgonzola cheese, crumbled

Directions
In a large pan, heat the grapeseed oil. Add the onion and cook over medium heat for about 3 minutes. Add the Brussels sprouts, thyme, salt and pepper. Cover and cook over moderate heat, stirring occasionally, until the sprouts are tender, about 3 minutes. Cover and remove from the heat.

Meanwhile, in a large pot of boiling, salted water, cook the penne until al dente. Drain, reserving 3/4 cup of the pasta water. Add the penne to the pan along with the pasta cooking water and cook over medium heat, mixing to blend the pasta with the vegetables. Transfer the pasta to bowls, top with the Gorgonzola and serve right away.

NUTRITION PER SERVING	Fats: 47g • Carbohydrates: 57g • Fiber: 5g Protein: 15g

Pesto Pasta With Broccoli
Serves 4

Ingredients
8 oz. organic brown rice elbow pasta
1 head fresh or frozen broccoli florets, cooked till tender
2 Tbsp. olive oil
Pink Himalayan sea salt and freshly ground black pepper, to taste
1/2 cup basil pesto (see recipe on next page)
1/3 cup sundried tomatoes, chopped

Directions
Preheat oven to 425 degrees. Lightly oil a baking sheet with grapeseed oil (wipe with paper towel).
Cook broccoli florets until tender.
Cook pasta according to package directions and drain.
In a large bowl, combine pasta, broccoli, pesto and sundried tomatoes.
Serve immediately.

Fat: 39g • Carbohydrates: 5g • Fiber: 1g
Protein: 7g

Basic Basil Pesto

Ingredients
2 bunches basil leaves
1/2 cup cashews
1/2 cup grated Parmesan cheese
3 garlic cloves
1/4 tsp. Pink Himalayan sea salt
1/2 cup extra-virgin olive oil

Directions
In a blender or food processor, blend 1 bunch of the basil with cashews, Parmesan and garlic. Blend until finely chopped.
Add in the rest of the basil and blend until a paste forms.
Pour in olive oil. Scrape down the sides of the bowl and continue blending as needed until the olive oil is absorbed into pesto.

NUTRITION PER SERVING | Fats: 7g • Carbohydrates: 31g • Fiber: 4g
Protein: 18g

Pineapple Chicken "Fried" Quinoa
Serves 3-4

Ingredients
1 cup uncooked quinoa
1 organic chicken breast, cut into bite-sized pieces – or use tofu, extra firm, cubed
1 cup crushed pineapple
2 eggs, beaten (optional)
3/4 cup mushrooms, chopped
3 Tbsp. low-sodium soy sauce or Bragg Liquid Aminos
3 green onions, thinly sliced
1 cup carrots, diced

Directions
Add 1 cup quinoa and 2 cups water to large saucepan.
Bring to boil, reduce heat and cover for 15 minutes.
Coat small pan with coconut oil and cook chicken.
(Skip next two steps if making Vegan option)

Coat another small pan with coconut oil and cook eggs without stirring.
Once solid, put eggs on cutting surface and chop.
Using egg pan, sauté mushrooms, green onions and carrots until tender.
Stir in quinoa, pineapple and egg pieces.
Add chicken to vegetable mixture.
Add soy sauce or spray with Bragg Liquid Aminos and stir. Serve hot.

Pineapple Chicken "Fried" Quinoa

Portabella Asparagus Risotto

NUTRITION PER SERVING | **Fats: 15g • Carbohydrates: 43g • Fiber: 10g
Protein: 10g**

Portabella Asparagus Risotto
Serves 4-6

Ingredients
4-5 cups low-sodium vegetable broth (you may have leftover broth at the end)
1 lb. asparagus, tough bottoms removed
1 sweet onion, diced
4 Tbsp. grapeseed oil
1 1/2 cups Portabella or crimini mushrooms, chopped
1 stalk celery, minced
3 garlic cloves, minced
1 cup short grain brown rice
sea salt & freshly ground black pepper, to taste
1 1/2 cups sweet peas
small handful baby spinach
1/3 cup nutritional yeast flakes (or Parmesan)
1/4 cup freshly chopped parsley
1 tsp. lemon zest (grated lemon peel)

Directions
Note: This whole process takes a little over an hour.
In a pan, sauté onion, celery, garlic and asparagus in grapeseed oil on medium heat for about 5 minutes. Add the mushrooms and cook another 2-3 minutes

until tender.

Now add the dry rice to the mixture and stir well for about 4 minutes.

Add 1/2 cup of broth. Sprinkle in salt and pepper and stir well.

Now reduce the heat and let mixture absorb the broth before adding another 1/2 cup of broth.

Repeat this process of adding 1/2 cup of broth 4 times (or as many times as it takes to soften rice). Let the mixture absorb the broth each time before adding more.

Finally, add in the sweet peas, spinach, parsley and lemon zest. Cook another 10 minutes, mixing constantly.

Rice should be tender at this point and risotto should have a creamy consistency.

Serve and enjoy!

NUTRITION PER SERVING | **Fats: 22g • Carbohydrates: 120g • Fiber: 15g**
Protein: 51g

Power Pasta Sauce
Serves 4-6

This sauce can be made several ways and can be mixed with everything or nothing. This sauce makes a great dip for bread, serve it over pasta or chicken, or mix with rice or quinoa for a hearty meal.

Ingredients
16 oz. pasta (whole wheat, durum, brown rice, quinoa or gluten-free pasta noodles)
4 16-oz. cans of diced tomatoes or 12-14 whole tomatoes, steamed, peeled & crushed
1 red pepper, chopped
1 green pepper, chopped
1 medium sweet onion, chopped
10-12 cloves garlic, diced
1 pinch each of basil, oregano & sea salt
16 oz. organic ground turkey (optional - not vegan)
extra virgin olive oil
grapeseed oil

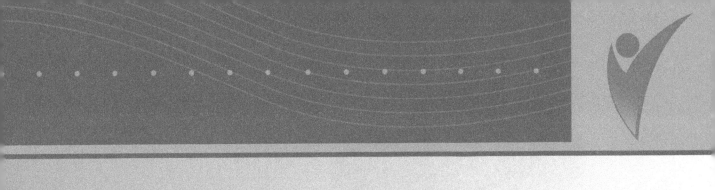

Directions

Pour diced tomatoes in large pot and heat over low-medium flame.

Add basil, oregano and sea salt before covering to simmer.

Sauté garlic, onion and peppers in grapeseed oil over low-medium heat.

In another pan at low-medium heat, begin to brown the turkey in grapeseed oil.

In another large pot, bring 6-8 cups water to boil.

Once vegetables have softened to your taste, add to sauce.

When turkey has thoroughly cooked, add to sauce, cover and simmer another 10 minutes before removing from heat.

Add pasta noodles to boiling water and cook for 8-12 minutes.

Stir in 2 Tbsp. extra virgin olive oil.

When noodles are done, add separately to plates and cover with sauce.

Power Pasta

Quinoa Stuffed Peppers

NUTRITION PER SERVING | **Fats: 27g • Carbohydrates: 62g • Fiber: 17g Protein: 16g**

Quinoa Stuffed Peppers
Serves 4-6

Ingredients
4 Tbsp. grapeseed oil
1 15-oz. can black beans
1 celery stalk, chopped
1 sweet onion, chopped
3 cloves garlic, minced
7 oz. Portabella mushrooms, chopped
6 green, red & yellow bell peppers (two peppers of each color)
5 oz. baby spinach
3/4 tsp. ground cumin
1 cup uncooked quinoa, cooked according to package directions
sea salt, to taste
ground pepper, to taste
1/2 cup pecans, crushed
1 Tbsp. honey - or agave
sprinkle of feta crumbles (optional)

Directions
Cook quinoa according to package directions and set aside.
Preheat oven to 350 degrees.

Using a paper towel, wipe a thin layer of grapeseed oil around a 9 x 12 casserole dish.

Slice peppers in half and remove the core and seeds. Lay peppers on their sides in casserole dish.

Next, heat grapeseed oil on low in large pan.

Add garlic, onion, celery and mushrooms. Cook about 8 minutes or until tender.

Add in spinach and allow to wilt. Then stir in cumin and cooked quinoa and mix well.

Now add salt, pepper and pecans and mix well for another minute.

Carefully stuff mixture into pepper halves and drizzle with honey. Cover with foil and bake 1 hour until peppers are soft.

Remove from oven and sprinkle with light layer of feta (optional).

Serve and enjoy!

NUTRITION PER SERVING | Fats: 29g • Carbohydrates: 80g • Fiber: 25g
Protein: 40g

Salmon, Green Beans & Avocado Bake
Serves 4

Ingredients
1 lb. fresh green beans, edges trimmed
2 Tbsp. grapeseed oil
1 Tbsp. extra virgin olive oil
dash of Pink Himalayan sea salt
dash of freshly ground black pepper
4 (6 oz.) boneless, skinless salmon filets
2 avocados, peeled & chopped
1 Tbsp. white wine vinegar
1 Tbsp. chopped fresh dill

Directions
Heat oven to 400 degrees. Mix the beans with 2 Tbsp. of grapeseed oil, and dash of salt and pepper in a casserole dish. Tuck the fish in the beans and bake until the beans are crisp-tender and the fish is just flaky throughout, about 8 minutes.
Meanwhile, combine the avocados, vinegar, dill, olive oil and dash of salt in a bowl.
Plate the fish and beans, and top with avocado mixture.

AVOCADO

Did you know that avocados can be used to replace virtually any fat source in baking? Try using it in place of oil or mayonnaise in cakes or try blending it with unsweetened cocoa for a healthy version of chocolate pudding.

NUTRITION PER SERVING | **Fat: 24g • Carbohydrates: 25g • Fiber: 5g
Protein: 61g**

Seared Ahi Tuna Steaks
Serves 2-4

Ingredients
1 lb. sashimi grade yellow fin tuna, cut into serving portions
sea salt, to taste
black pepper, to taste
1/2 cup oat bran or buckwheat
1 Tbsp. Italian seasoning
3 Tbsp. grapeseed oil

Directions
Roll the tuna in the oat bran or buckwheat and the sprinkle with salt, pepper and Italian seasoning.
Drizzle grapeseed oil in large pan and put on high heat.
Place the tuna in the pan, searing it on all sides (about 30-40 seconds per side).
Remove from pan and plate.
Pair with your favorite sides or put on top of leafy green salad and enjoy!

Shells With Minty Pistachio Pesto
Serves 6

Ingredients
7 oz. unsalted roasted shelled pistachios (1 1/2 cups)
1/2 cup extra-virgin olive oil
2 Tbsp. chopped mint
1 garlic clove, minced
1/2 cup finely shredded pecorino cheese, plus more for serving
2 scallions, cut into 2-inch lengths and julienned
dash of salt
1 lb. small shell pasta

Directions
In a food processor, chop the pistachios. Add the olive oil, mint and garlic, and pulse to combine. Transfer to a bowl, and stir in the 1/2 cup of cheese and the scallions; season with salt.
In a large pot of salted boiling water, cook the pasta until al dente; drain, reserving 1/2 cup of the cooking water. Return the pasta to the pot. Add the cooking water and the pesto and cook over low heat, tossing, until coated. Serve.

NUTRITION PER SERVING | Fats: 11g • Carbohydrates: 26g • Fiber: 7g
Protein: 46g

Skinny Sumo Stir-Fry
Serves 1-2

Ingredients
1 chicken breast, cut into bite-sized pieces – or serve over quinoa instead (vegan)
2 cups broccoli, chopped
1 cup mushrooms, chopped
1 Tbsp. low-sodium soy sauce or 2 sprays of Bragg Liquid Aminos
4 green onions, chopped
handful bean sprouts

Directions
Coat small pan with peanut oil and cook chicken until no longer pink inside.
Steam broccoli in separate pan until tender.
In another pan, sauté mushrooms in peanut oil until browned.
Combine chicken, mushrooms and broccoli in bowl.
Top with onions, sprouts and low-sodium soy sauce.

Skinny Sumo Stir-Fry shown here topped with sriracha sauce

NUTRITION
PER SERVING | Fats: 8g • Carbohydrates: 44g • Fiber: 8g
Protein: 24g

Slightly Sloppy Mikes
Serves 4

Ingredients
whole wheat or gluten-free buns (regular bread slices will do just fine, too!)
1/2 lb. organic ground turkey
1 small onion, finely chopped
2 cloves garlic, minced
1 green bell pepper, diced
1/2 cup pinto beans
1/2 cup black beans
1 cup diced tomatoes
1/2 Tbsp. tomato paste
1/2 Tbsp. apple cider vinegar
1 Tbsp. maple syrup
1 Tbsp. Worcestershire sauce
1 Tbsp. spicy mustard
dash of sea salt
dash of black pepper
1 jalapeño pepper, minced (optional)

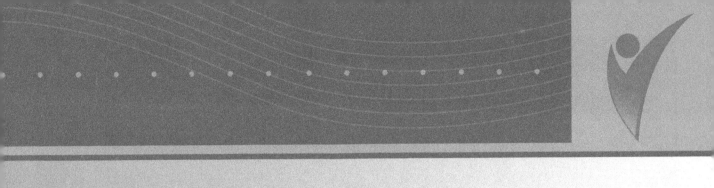

Directions

Cook turkey meat on medium heat for about 10 minutes until done.

In separate, large pan, sauté onion, garlic, green pepper and jalapeño until soft.

Add meat to the veggie pan along with rest of ingredients and reduce heat to a simmer, stirring occasionally.

Once thickened, scoop onto bread of your choice and serve.

This can also be eaten breadless in a bowl!

NUTRITION PER SERVING | **Fats: 15g • Carbohydrates: 75g • Fiber: 13g Protein: 14g**

Smoked Veggie Paella
Serves 4-6

Ingredients
5 cloves garlic, minced
7 oz. Portabella mushrooms, chopped
2 large bunches chard, leaves pulled from center stem & chopped
1 large yellow onion, chopped
5 whole artichoke hearts (canned in water is fine), cut into quarters
1 cup black rice, dry (a short grain brown rice, or quinoa works well, too)
4 1/2 cups low-sodium vegetable broth (keep some extra on the side)
4-5 vine-ripened tomatoes, seeded & diced
1 1/2 cups chickpeas, drained
3 Tbsp. grapeseed oil
1 Tbsp. smoked paprika
1 tsp. turmeric
sea salt, to taste
ground pepper, to taste

Directions
Drizzle extra large pan with grapeseed oil.
Sauté garlic and onions for about 5 minutes over medium heat until tender and then toss in the mushrooms and sauté until brown.

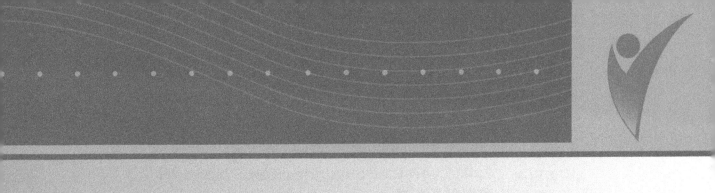

Add the uncooked rice to the pan and stir well.

Now add the tomatoes, chard, chickpeas, salt, pepper, turmeric and smoked paprika. Stir well for about a minute.

Pour in enough vegetable broth to cover the entire mixture and layer artichoke hearts on top. They'll eventually fall apart when you mix the paella later.

Reduce heat to a simmer and cover. Let cook about 40 minutes before uncovering and cooking another 15-20 minutes until rice is tender. As it cooks, you'll need to add more broth to the mixture so keep it at the ready!

Once it's done, set aside about 10-15 minutes and then serve.

NUTRITION
PER SERVING | Fats: 25g • Carbohydrates: 23g • Fiber: 7g
Protein: 42g

Smoky Roasted Chicken Breasts With Chickpeas, Tomatoes & Cilantro
Serves 4-5

Ingredients
5 Tbsp. grapeseed oil
4 garlic cloves, minced
1 Tbsp. smoked paprika
1 tsp. sweet paprika
1 tsp. ground cumin
2 tsp. salt, divided
1 tsp. freshly ground black pepper
1/2 tsp. crushed red pepper
1 cup Greek yogurt
4 large chicken breasts, with skin
2 cups cherry tomatoes
1 (15 oz.) can chickpeas, drained and rinsed
1 cup fresh cilantro

Directions
Heat oven to 450 degrees.

Whisk oil, garlic, paprikas, cumin, 1 tsp. salt, pepper and crushed red pepper in a small bowl. Transfer 1 Tbsp. of the oil to another bowl and whisk in the yogurt. Set aside until serving.

Place chicken in a large casserole dish and brush with oil. Place tomatoes, chickpeas and half of the cilantro in a bowl. Add remaining oil and stir to coat. Pour into the casserole dish around the chicken. Turn to coat the chicken with any extra oil. Be sure to keep the skin side up for roasting. Sprinkle with 1 tsp. Pink Himalayan sea salt.

Roast chicken in oven until cooked through, 20-30 minutes. Transfer chicken to serving plates or a platter and spoon the beans and tomatoes over. Garnish with cilantro and serve with yogurt sauce.

NUTRITION PER SERVING | **Fats: 12g • Carbohydrates: 83g • Fiber: 9g**
Protein: 33g

Spinach & Mushroom Lasagna
Serves 4-6

Ingredients
1/2 lb. fresh mushrooms, sliced
1 tsp. chopped garlic
1/2 yellow onion, chopped
2 Tbsp. water
2 24-oz. jars of diced tomatoes
9-12 lasagna noodles (regular or no-boil is fine, uncooked)
Note: DeBoles makes a gluten-free rice lasagna.
2 Tbsp. grapeseed oil
5 oz. fresh baby spinach (about 2-3 large handfuls)
1 lb. cottage cheese
2 Tbsp. nutritional yeast (or Parmesan)
1/2 cup fresh mozzarella, shredded (optional)
1/2 tsp. garlic powder
2 Tbsp. Italian seasoning

Directions
Preheat oven to 350 degrees.
Sauté the mushrooms, onion and garlic over medium heat in grapeseed oil until tender. Add in spinach. When it begins to wilt, reduce heat to low and

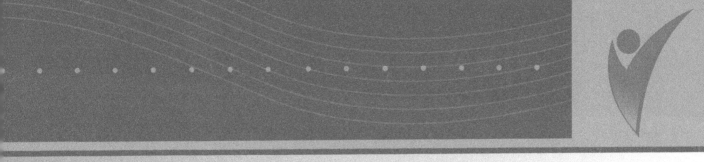

add tomatoes, stirring often. Cook about 3 minutes and set aside, covered.

In a large bowl, combine cottage cheese, nutritional yeast, Italian seasonings and garlic powder and mix well.

Spread a thin layer of tomato sauce in the bottom of a lasagna pan. This is our foundation.

Now place 3-4 lasagna noodles over the sauce. The noodles shouldn't overlap.

Next, spread a thin layer of cottage cheese mixture over the noodles.

Cover with another layer of 3-4 noodles followed by another layer of sauce and then another layer of cottage cheese. You should end up with a layer of noodles on top.

Spread the remaining tomato sauce on the top layer of noodles and sprinkle a few shakes of Italian seasoning on top.

Cover with aluminum foil, and bake for 40 minutes.

Remove the foil and sprinkle Parmesan or shredded mozzarella on top and bake uncovered for another 20 minutes.

Wait about 10-15 minutes before serving. Enjoy!

NUTRITION
PER SERVING | **Fats: 10g • Carbohydrates: 87g • Fiber: 11g**
Protein: 18g

Spinach Pasta
Serves 4-6

Ingredients
16 oz. whole wheat or brown rice noodles, or 1 cup quinoa
handful fresh baby spinach
1 cup basil leaves, tightly packed
3 cloves garlic, minced
1 Tbsp. grapeseed oil
1/3 cup almond milk
1/2 cup mozzarella cheese, shredded (optional – not vegan)
dash pink Himalayan sea salt & pepper to taste

Directions
Cook pasta (or quinoa) according to package directions.
Chop spinach and basil in blender or food processor. If you don't have a chopping appliance, just shred by hand.
In a large saucepan, sauté garlic in grapeseed oil.
Add milk and spinach mixture to saucepan. Bring to a boil, then reduce heat to a simmer. Stir occasionally until sauce slightly thickens and remove from heat.
Drain water and add noodles to spinach mixture in saucepan. Add cheese, sea salt and pepper. Serve immediately.

NUTRITION PER SERVING | **Fats: 33g • Carbohydrates: 21g • Fiber: 7g
Protein: 60g**

Steak & Asparagus
Serves 2-4

Ingredients
3 Tbsp. grapeseed oil
4 cloves garlic, minced
1 large sirloin steak, cut into 1/2 inch cubes
3-4 sprays of Bragg Liquid Aminos or 1 Tbsp. low-sodium soy sauce
1 medium yellow onion, diced
2 stalks celery, diced
5 oz. crimini mushrooms, sliced
1 lb. asparagus, each spear chopped into 1/2-inch bites
1/2 cup water

Directions
Heat grapeseed oil in a large pan over medium heat and spray steak with Bragg Liquid Aminos or low-sodium soy sauce. Cook until steak is browned on all sides, about 3 minutes. Turn off heat and set aside.
In separate pan, add garlic, onion, celery and sliced asparagus. Sauté 2 minutes and add steak into mixture. Add water and cover pan. Cook about 5 minutes or until asparagus is tender and steak pieces are cooked through. Enjoy!

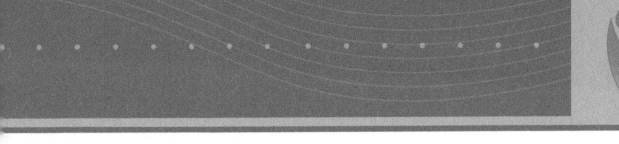

FOOD | FACTOIDS

ASPARAGUS

When storing asparagus, wrap the ends of the stem in damp paper towels for a few days, or to prolong freshness, soak stems in a cup of shallow water standing upright.

NUTRITION
PER SERVING

Fats: 9g • Carbohydrates: 38g • Fiber: 9g
Protein: 8g

Stuffed Cabbage Flytraps
Serves 5-6

Ingredients
1/2 cup quinoa, cooked according to package directions
1 head of cabbage
1 small onion, diced
2-3 Tbsp. organic maple syrup
1/2 red pepper, diced
1/2 green pepper, diced
large handful baby spinach
2 cloves garlic, minced
1 (15-oz.) can of red beans (or black beans), drained
2 (15-oz.) can diced tomatoes, drained
sea salt, to taste
black pepper, to taste
2 Tbsp. nutritional yeast (or Parmesan) (optional)
4 oz. crimini or Portabella mushrooms
3 Tbsp. grapeseed oil
4 tsp. dried basil

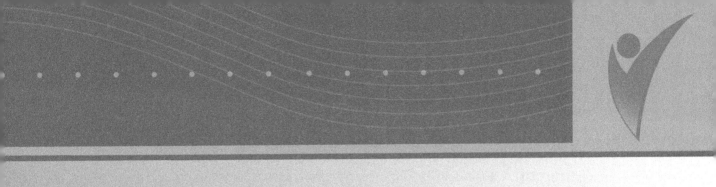

Directions

Preheat oven to 350 degrees.

Cook the quinoa before everything else so it's ready when you go to stuff the cabbage leaves, and set aside.

Sauté the onion, garlic and peppers in grapeseed oil on medium heat until tender. Add in mushrooms and spinach and mix well. Cook another 2-3 minutes until mushrooms are browned and spinach is wilted.

Mix the beans, quinoa, salt, pepper and nutritional yeast (or Parmesan) into the onion mixture and stir well until everything is heated through, and set aside.

Now bring a large pot of water to a boil (big enough to fit the head of cabbage). Core (cut out the center) of the cabbage and throw away. Place cabbage head in the boiling water. This will allow for easy stuffing of the leaves. Let boil about 2 minutes and remove from heat.

For the sauce: In a bowl, mix the tomatoes together with maple syrup and basil. Add about 1/4 cup of the sauce to the quinoa mixture and mix.

Now remove the leaves and stuff each one with about 1/4 to 1/2 cup of the quinoa mixture depending on how large the cabbage leaf. Fold the cabbage leaf ends around the mixture and place seam-side down in a 9 x 12 casserole dish.

Pour remaining sauce over the cabbage rolls and cover. Bake for about 45-50 minutes.

NUTRITION
PER SERVING | **Fats: 46g • Carbohydrates: 33g • Fiber: 8g**
Protein: 5g

Sweet Citrus Spinach Salad
Serves 2-4

Ingredients
5 oz. (or 2 large handfuls) baby spinach
1/2 cucumber, peeled & sliced into rounds
5-6 mandarin oranges, peeled & divided
1/2 cup pine nuts
1/4 cup apple cider vinegar
1/2 cup extra virgin olive oil
1 Tbsp. agave & drizzle of agave for pine nuts (or honey)
dash of black pepper

Directions
Divide spinach, cucumber and mandarin oranges among serving bowls.
Add pine nuts to small pan and lightly drizzle with agave. Toast pine nuts for
about 1-2 minutes, stirring constantly. Set aside when done.
Whisk together apple cider vinegar, olive oil, 1 Tbsp. agave and black pepper in
a small bowl and drizzle over salad. Add pine nuts to the tops of each salad.

NUTRITION
PER SERVING

**Fats: 53g • Carbohydrates: 26g • Fiber: 9g
Protein: 10g**

Tangy Beet & Spinach Salad
Serves 2-4

Ingredients
6 beets
1 Tbsp. grapeseed oil
3 Tbsp. extra virgin olive oil
1 Tbsp. apple cider vinegar
4-5 oz. baby spinach
1/2 cup pecans roughly chopped & toasted
2 oz. goat cheese or feta (optional)
dash of black pepper

Directions
Preheat oven to 450 degrees.
Preparing beets: Trim stems and root. Wash and pat dry. Place in baking dish, brush with grapeseed oil and cover tightly with 2 layers of aluminum foil. Bake for 1 hour. Beets should be tender when done. Allow to cool to room temperature before scraping off beet skin with paring knife. Cut beets into bite-sized pieces. Add beets to a large bowl along with spinach and pecans and mix well. Separate into serving bowls.
In another small bowl, blend olive oil, apple cider vinegar and a little black pepper. Drizzle over each salad. Top with goat cheese or feta.
Enjoy!

Thoro-Breaded "Fried" Chicken
Serves 1-2

Ingredients
1 chicken breast, sliced horizontally
1 cup oat bran or buckwheat (gluten-free option)
1 egg
1/3 cup almond milk
1 Tbsp. ground flax seeds

Directions
Mix 1 egg and 1/3 cup milk in small bowl.
Combine oat bran and flax seeds in separate bowl.
Coat pan with coconut oil and heat over low-medium flame.
Dip chicken in egg/milk mixture, and then roll chicken in oat bran/flax seeds mixture to coat.
Immediately place in pan. Cook 3-4 minutes on each side.

NUTRITION PER SERVING | Fats: 16g • Carbohydrates: 14g • Fiber: 3g
Protein: 37g

Turkey Burgers
Serves 2

Ingredients
1/2 lb. lean turkey
1/4 cup oat bran or buckwheat (G)
1 whole egg
2 cloves garlic, chopped
1 tsp. Worcestershire or teriyaki sauce
dash each of sea salt, pepper & oregano
Optional toppings:
Romaine lettuce
sliced tomato
dill pickle
avocado
cheese
ketchup
mustard

Directions
Lightly coat pan with grapeseed oil and set on low-medium heat.
In a large bowl, combine everything except toppings and mix well.
Shape into 4 to 5 palm-sized patties.

Place patties in pan and flatten with spatula.
Grill, covered, over indirect medium heat for 4-6 minutes on each side or until meat is no longer pink inside.
Serve on bread or wrapped in lettuce with optional toppings.

NUTRITION
PER SERVING | Fats: 30g • Carbohydrates: 69g • Fiber: 10g
Protein: 47g

Turkey Meatballs
Serves 4-6

Note: This recipe is similar to the Meatless Meatballs, but here we use ground turkey instead of beans and we pan fry them in grapeseed oil.

Ingredients
16 oz. spaghetti (use your favorite kind). Cook and set aside.

For the meatballs:
4 Tbsp. grapeseed oil
1 small onion, chopped
5 oz. crimini mushrooms, chopped (optional)
1 tsp. black pepper
1/4 tsp. salt
1 lb. ground turkey
3 garlic cloves, chopped
2 Tbsp. Worcestershire sauce
1/2 cup fresh parsley, chopped
1 cup oat bran (or buckwheat)
1/4 cup grated Parmesan or nutritional yeast

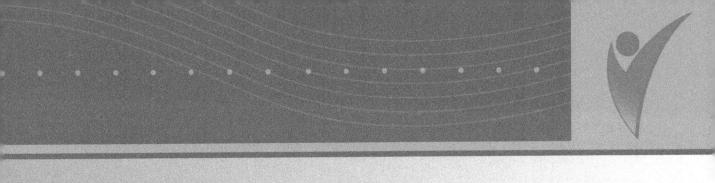

Directions

Heat grapeseed oil in large skillet on a low heat.

Combine all ingredients in a large bowl and mix well to form a thick batter.

Form 2-inch meatballs with your hands and place in pan with oil.

Cook on all sides until outside is browned and inside is cooked through, about 10 minutes total. (Cut one open to be sure.)

Add the meatballs to your favorite pasta and sauce.

(Hint: These go great with the Power Pasta recipe!)

Enjoy!

SIDES & SNACKS

NUTRITION PER SERVING | Fats: 15g • Carbohydrates: 31g • Fiber: 4g
Protein: 5g

Angry Steve's Potato Salad
Serves 8

Ingredients
6 organic red potatoes
3 stalks celery, diced
1 large onion, diced
1/4 cup mustard seed
dash of Pink Himalayan sea salt
dash of freshly ground black pepper
dash of garlic powder
3/4 cup organic Vegenaise, to taste
(optional garnish: 1/4 cup fresh parsley)

Directions
Boil potatoes until soft but not mushy. Drain and run under cold water. Add potatoes to large mixing bowl and mash.
Add celery and onion to potatoes. Mix in mustard seed, salt, pepper and garlic powder to taste. Mix in Vegenaise. Garnish with parsley if desired and serve.

Apple & Honey GO Bars
Serves 3

Ingredients
1 apple
1 cup dates
1/4 cup pecans
1 tsp. cinnamon
1 tsp. nutmeg
1 Tbsp. honey (optional)
1/4 cup ground flaxseed

Directions
First, lay out three 12 x 12 pieces of plastic wrap.
Next, put apples and dates in your food processor or blender and blend until a paste forms. Put in bowl and set aside.
Now add the pecans to the blender and chop them up.
Add the nuts, cinnamon, nutmeg, flaxseed and honey to the bowl with the apple mixture and with a wooden spoon (or your fingers) mush the mixture together until well blended.
Divide the mixture into thirds and place in each of the three pieces of plastic wrap laid out earlier and wrap up the mixture tightly.
Shape the mixture into bars (a rolling pin helps) and keep wrapped.
Refrigerate for about an hour and they're ready to eat!

NUTRITION PER SERVING | **Fats: 14g • Carbohydrates: 15g • Fiber: 3g Protein: 4g**

Apricot & Nut GO Bars
Serves 3

Ingredients
3/4 cup apricots
1/4 cup dates, chopped
1/4 cup pecans
1/4 cup walnuts
1/2 tsp. cinnamon
1 tsp. maple syrup (optional)
1 tsp. ground flaxseed

Directions
First, lay out three 12 x 12 pieces of plastic wrap.
Next, put apricots and dates in your food processor or blender and blend until a paste forms. Put in bowl and set aside.
Now add the nuts to the blender and chop them up.
Add the nuts, cinnamon, flaxseed and syrup to the bowl with the apricot mixture and with a wooden spoon (or your fingers) mush the mixture together until well blended.
Divide the mixture into thirds and place in each of the three pieces of plastic wrap laid out earlier and wrap up the mixture tightly.
Shape the mixture into bars (a rolling pin helps) and keep wrapped.
Refrigerate for about an hour and they're ready to eat!

Baked Avocado Fries
Serves 2-4

Ingredients
2 avocados, peeled & sliced
Add a pinch of the following spices in a small bowl & blend:
sea salt
black pepper
onion powder
turmeric (optional)
chili (or cayenne powder)

Directions
Preheat oven to 375 degrees.
Put avocados on a baking tray lined with foil.
Sprinkle the seasoning over the avocado slices.
Put the trays into the oven and bake for 10 minutes.
Remove from oven and flip each one carefully. Add some seasoning to the naked sides of the avocados and bake for about 20 minutes or until outsides get a bit crispy.
When they're done, sprinkle a little more seasoning on them, to taste.
Serve alone, as a snack or as a side.

NUTRITION
PER SERVING

**Fats: 3.5g • Carbohydrates: 30g • Fiber: 4g
Protein: 3g**

Baked Fingerling Potatoes
Serves 4

Ingredients
1 Tbsp. grapeseed oil
1 1/2 lbs. fingerling potatoes
dash of Pink Himalayan sea salt
dash of black pepper
dash of ground red pepper

Directions
Preheat oven to 400 degrees.
Coat potatoes with grapeseed oil and place on baking sheet. Sprinkle with salt and both black and red peppers. Bake for 30 minutes or until tender.

Blood Orange Salad
Serves 6

Ingredients
4 blood oranges, peeled and divided into slices
1/2 cup red onion, sliced
dash of Pink Himalayan sea salt
dash of freshly ground black pepper
dash of ground red pepper
2 Tbsp. extra virgin olive oil

Directions
Arrange orange slices on a large dish. Top evenly with onion. Sprinkle with salt, black pepper and red pepper. Drizzle with oil. Serve immediately.

NUTRITION PER SERVING | Fats: 12g • Carbohydrates: 46g • Fiber: 5g
Protein: 7g

Blueberry & Date GO Bars
Serves 3

Ingredients
1 1/2 cups fresh blueberries
1 tsp. fresh lemon juice
1/2 tsp. lemon zest
1 cup dates
1/4 cup pecans
1 tsp. cinnamon
1 Tbsp. honey (optional)
1/4 cup ground flaxseed

Directions
First, lay out three 12 x 12 pieces of plastic wrap.

Next, put all ingredients except the blueberries in a food processor or blender and blend until a paste forms. Put paste in bowl and add blueberries.

With a wooden spoon (or your fingers) mush the mixture together until well blended.

Divide the mixture into thirds and place in each of the three pieces of plastic wrap laid out earlier and wrap up the mixture tightly.

Shape the mixture into bars (a rolling pin helps) and keep wrapped.

Refrigerate for about an hour and they're ready to eat!

CINNAMON

Cinnamon increases insulin production in the body, therefore, helping to keep blood sugars low. It also acts as a natural preservative to prevent spoilage and bacterial growth when sprinkled on foods.

NUTRITION PER SERVING | Fats: 2g • Carbohydrates: 35g • Fiber: 3g
Protein: 19g

Blueberry Madness
Serves 1

Ingredients
6 oz. plain Greek yogurt
1/2 cup blueberries
1 Tbsp. agave or honey
1 tsp. chia seed

Directions
Combine all ingredients in bowl and enjoy!

NUTRITION PER SERVING | **Fats: 14g • Carbohydrates: 24g • Fiber: 7g Protein: 6g**

Brussels Sprouts With Pomegranate & Cashews
Serves 4

Ingredients
1 lb. Brussels sprouts, trimmed and halved
1/2 cup cashews
1- 1 1/2 cups pomegranate seeds
2 Tbsp. grapeseed oil
dash of Pink Himalayan sea salt
1 Tbsp. Bragg Liquid Aminos
dash of freshly ground pepper

Directions
Preheat oven to 375 degrees.
Put the Brussels sprouts in a medium roasting pan; toss with the grapeseed oil and season with salt and pepper. Roast for about 45 minutes or until sprouts are tender. Remove sprouts from oven and put in large bowl with pomegranate seeds, 1 Tbsp. Bragg Liquid Aminos and cashews. Lightly stir, then serve immediately.

Butter-Pecan Jasmine Rice
Serves 2-4

Ingredients
1 cup brown Jasmine rice
1 Tbsp. grass-fed butter
1/4 cup pecans, chopped
dash of Pink Himalayan sea salt

Directions
In a small pot, cook rice according to package directions. However, don't add salt or butter if rice directions call for it.

Then, in a separate pot, melt 1 Tbsp. butter over medium heat; cook for about 3 minutes or until browned. Lower heat to a simmer and add pecans. Cook for about 2 minutes until toasted, stirring often. Add rice to pecan mixture. Add dash of salt. Stir well and serve.

NUTRITION PER SERVING | **Fats: 6g • Carbohydrates: 27g • Fiber: 3g Protein: 2g**

Candied Acorn Squash
Serves 2

Ingredients
1 acorn squash
1 Tbsp. grass-fed butter, melted
2 tsp. organic maple syrup
dash of coconut sugar

Directions
Preheat oven to 400 degrees.

Cut the acorn squash in half and scoop out seeds and strings.

Scrape out the seeds and stringy pieces.

With a sharp knife, create a cross-hatch pattern on the inside of each squash, about a half-inch deep.

Place the squash halves cut side up in a roasting pan. Pour 1/4 inch of water over the bottom of the pan. Brush the inside of each squash with melted grass-fed butter. Sprinkle with coconut sugar and maple syrup. Bake for about an hour until squash is browned and squash flesh is very soft. Remove from oven and spoon any maple syrup pooled in the center of the squash over the top. Serve warm.

NUTRITION PER SERVING | Fats: 0g • Carbohydrates: 21g • Fiber: 3g
Protein: 2g

Candied Baby Carrots
Serves 2-3

Ingredients
2 cups organic baby carrots
1/2 cup orange juice (fresh squeezed if possible)
1 cup water
1 tsp. maple syrup or agave (optional)

Directions
Boil water and orange juice together in a small pot and add in carrots.
Cook about 10 minutes or until carrots are tender.
Drain carrots and serve. (You can also drizzle with maple syrup or agave
before serving.)

NUTRITION PER SERVING | Fats: 14g • Carbohydrates: 19g • Fiber: 3g
Protein: 3g

Cherry & Nut GO Bars
Serves 3

Ingredients
1/2 cup chopped dates (try to get from your produce section - if you have to get pre-packaged dates, wash them in warm water before using to help get rid of any preservative)
1/2 cup cherries, pitted & chopped
1/2 cup pecans
1/2 tsp. cinnamon
1 tsp. maple syrup (optional)
1 tsp. ground flaxseed

Directions
First, lay out three 12 x 12 pieces of plastic wrap.
Next, put dates and cherries in your food processor or blender and blend until a paste forms. Put in bowl and set aside.
Now add the nuts to the blender and chop them up.
Add the nuts, cinnamon, flaxseed and syrup to the bowl with the cherries and with a wooden spoon (or your fingers) mush the mixture together until well blended.

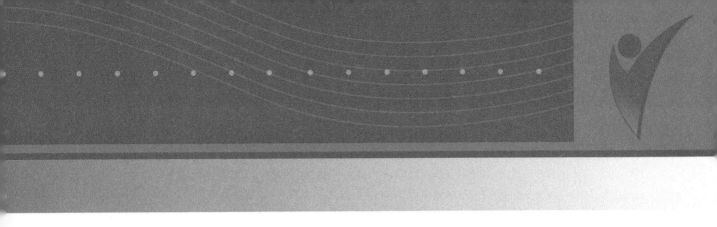

Divide the mixture into thirds and place in each of the three pieces of plastic wrap laid out earlier and wrap up the mixture tightly.
Shape the mixture into bars (a rolling pin helps) and keep wrapped.
Refrigerate for about an hour and they're ready to eat!

NUTRITION PER SERVING | **Fats: 13g • Carbohydrates: 41g • Fiber: 4g Protein: 7g**

Cranberry, Raisin & Peanut GO Bars
Serves 3

Ingredients
1/2 cup raisins
1/2 cup dried cranberries
1/2 cup peanuts, unsalted
1 tsp. maple syrup (optional)
1 tsp. ground flaxseed

Directions
First, lay out three 12 x 12 pieces of plastic wrap.
Next, put raisins and cranberries in your food processor or blender and blend until a paste forms. Put in bowl and set aside.
Now add the nuts to the blender and chop them up.
Add the nuts, flaxseed and syrup to the bowl with the raisins and with a wooden spoon (or your fingers) mush the mixture together until well blended.
Divide the mixture into thirds and place in each of the three pieces of plastic wrap laid out earlier and wrap up the mixture tightly.
Shape the mixture into bars (a rolling pin helps) and keep wrapped.
Refrigerate for about an hour and they're ready to eat!

NUTRITION PER SERVING	Fats: 0.5g • Carbohydrates: 26g • Fiber: 5g Protein: 1g

Crunchy Apple Crisps
Serves 1

Ingredients
apples, thinly sliced, dash of cinnamon, dash of nutmeg

Directions
Heat oven to 225 degrees. Place apple slices in a single layer on a baking sheet covered in parchment paper. Sprinkle with cinnamon and nutmeg. Bake in oven for 1 hour. Flip apple slices over, then bake for another hour. Allow to cool about 15-20 minutes. Enjoy.

NUTRITION
PER SERVING

Fats: 0g • Carbohydrates: 62g • Fiber: 10g
Protein: 13g

Easy Baked Beans
Serves 2-3

Ingredients
15 oz. cannellini beans, drained & rinsed
3 Tbsp. ketchup
2 Tbsp. Dijon mustard
3 Tbsp. organic maple syrup
1 tsp. smoked paprika

Directions
Preheat oven to 350 degrees.
Combine all ingredients together and bake in casserole dish 30 minutes or until bubbling.

Fresh Salsa
Serves 2-4

Ingredients
3 medium tomatoes, chopped
1/2 red onion, finely diced
2 small cloves of garlic, minced
1 lime, juiced
1/2 cup chopped cilantro
salt & pepper to taste
few sprinkles of oregano
1 jalapeño chili pepper, diced (optional)

Directions
Combine all of the ingredients in a bowl.
Taste, and season to your liking.
Refrigerate for an hour and serve with your favorite sea-salted pita chips or homemade tortilla chips - recipes for these are in this book!

NUTRITION PER SERVING | Fats: 6g • Carbohydrates: 15g • Fiber: 5g
Protein: 6g

Garlic Snow Peas
Serves 1-2

Ingredients
2 cups fresh snow peas
1 Tbsp. toasted sesame seeds
2 minced garlic cloves
2 Tbsp. grapeseed oil
dash of sea salt
dash of black pepper

Directions
In medium pan, sauté snow peas in grapeseed oil about 5 minutes or until bright green.
Add in garlic, sesame seeds, and salt and pepper.
Serve and enjoy!

NUTRITION
PER SERVING | **Fats: 1g • Carbohydrates: 47g • Fiber: 6g**
Protein: 1g

Gram's Baked Apples
Serves 2-4

Ingredients
4 large apples
3/4 cup plain almond milk
sprinkle of Saigon cinnamon
sprinkle of nutmeg
drizzle of organic maple syrup
1/2 cup golden raisins

Directions
Preheat oven to 375 degrees.
Slice apples in half. Clean out the seeds and hard center. Place in baking dish.
Coat in maple syrup and then almond milk.
Add in raisins.
Sprinkle with cinnamon and nutmeg.
Bake 40 minutes while intermittently basting apples with the milk/syrup mixture from bottom of baking dish. The apples are done when a fork easily pierces the apple.
Remove from oven and let cool about 10 minutes.
Place apples in bowls and spoon the almond/maple syrup mixture over the apples again in the bowls. Be sure to get the raisins, too!
You can always add more almond milk/syrup to taste.
Enjoy!

Henrietta's Bruschetta
Serves 2-4

Ingredients
4 vine-ripened tomatoes, seeded & diced
1/2 red pepper, diced
2 cloves garlic, minced
1 tsp. grapeseed oil
1 Tbsp. extra virgin olive oil
1 tsp. balsamic vinegar
1/4 cup fresh basil, minced
sea salt, to taste
pepper, to taste
1/4 cup fresh mozzarella, shredded (optional)
whole wheat or gluten-free baguette, sliced

Directions
Preheat oven to 350 degrees.
Combine red pepper, tomatoes, basil, sea salt, pepper, mozzarella and garlic in bowl and toss with olive oil. Refrigerate about 30 minutes until chilled.
Meanwhile, slice bread and place on baking sheet. Brush with grapeseed oil and bake 5-8 minutes until lightly toasted.
Top with tomato mixture and serve immediately.

NUTRITION PER SERVING | **Fats: 14g • Carbohydrates: 44g • Fiber: 6g Protein: 8g**

Homebaked Tortilla Chips
Serves 2-4

Ingredients
gluten-free tortillas cut into triangles
1 Tbsp. grapeseed oil
dash of sea salt

Directions
Preheat oven to 350 degrees.
Place tortilla pieces on baking sheet and brush with grapeseed oil.
Sprinkle with salt.
Bake about 8 minutes until crisp.
Serve and enjoy!

NUTRITION
PER SERVING

Fats: 4g • Carbohydrates: 15g • Fiber: 1g
Protein: 1g

Homemade Dipping Chips
Serves 4

Ingredients
1/2 cup rice flour
1 Tbsp. extra virgin olive oil
1/2 cup water
1/4 tsp. Pink Himalayan sea salt

Directions
Heat oven to 400 degrees.
Blend together rice flour and oil, then stir in water.
Drop tsp. of batter onto a greased baking sheet, keeping space between drops.
Bake for about 12 minutes or until browned.
Remove from oven and sprinkle some salt on top. Enjoy!

NUTRITION PER SERVING | **Fats: 14g • Carbohydrates: 44g • Fiber: 6g**
Protein: 8g

Italian Tortilla Chips
Serves 2-4

Ingredients
gluten-free tortillas, cut into triangles
1 Tbsp. grapeseed oil
dash of Italian seasoning
sprinkle of Parmesan or nutritional yeast
dash of sea salt

Directions
Preheat oven to 350 degrees.
Place tortilla pieces on baking sheet and brush with grapeseed oil.
Sprinkle with salt, Italian seasoning and Parmesan (or nutritional yeast).
Bake about 8 minutes until crisp.
Serve and enjoy!

Kiwi Mango Chia Pudding
Serves 1

Ingredients
1/4 cup chia seed
1/4 cup water
1/2 mango, diced
1 kiwi, diced
1 tsp. agave

Directions
Combine chia seed and water in small bowl and let sit for about an hour until thick and pudding-like.
Top with kiwi and mango.
Drizzle with agave and serve.

NUTRITION PER SERVING | Fats: 0g • Carbohydrates: 44g • Fiber: 4g
Protein: 4g

Mashed Sweet Potatoes
Serves 2-3

Ingredients
2 large sweet potatoes
3 Tbsp. almond milk
2 Tbsp. plain Greek yogurt or soy yogurt (both optional)
2 Tbsp. agave
dash of cinnamon
dash of sea salt

Directions
Wash and peel potatoes and cut into hunks.
Boil large pot of water and add potatoes. Cook about 20-30 minutes until a fork easily goes through them.
Drain water.
Mash potatoes in the pot and add the rest of the ingredients, mixing well. If you have an electric beater, you can use that to make them extra creamy, but a fork or potato masher will do just fine.
Serve and enjoy!

NUTRITION
PER SERVING

Fats: 23g • Carbohydrates: 39g • Fiber: 2g
Protein: 6g

Minty Watermelon Salad
Serves 6

Ingredients
1 (6 lbs.) watermelon, chopped into bite-sized pieces
1 sweet onion, chopped
1/4 cup red wine vinegar
dash of Pink Himalayan sea salt
dash of freshly ground black pepper
1/2 cup extra virgin olive oil
2 Tbsp. mint, chopped
4 oz. feta cheese, crumbled

Directions
In a small bowl, whisk together the vinegar, salt and pepper.
Next, mix in the olive oil and mint.

In a separate large bowl, combine the melon, onion and crumbled feta. Pour the dressing over the melon and carefully toss until well mixed. Serve and enjoy!

Muscle Sprouts
Serves 2-4

Ingredients
14-20 Brussels sprouts, halved
4 Tbsp. grapeseed oil
4-5 sprays of Bragg Liquid Aminos, or a tsp. of low-sodium soy sauce

Directions
Heat grapeseed oil in large pan over medium heat.
Add Brussels sprouts, flat sides down and cook until browned, then flip and brown other side.
Transfer Brussels sprouts to serving dish and spray with Bragg Liquid Aminos (or low-sodium soy sauce).

NUTRITION
PER SERVING

Fats: 21g • Carbohydrates: 21g • Fiber: 5g
Protein: 6g

Mushroom & Pine Nut Fried Brown Rice
Serves 4

Ingredients
1 cup brown rice, cooked according to package directions
1 Tbsp. peanut oil
1/2 cup onion, sliced thin
1 tsp. minced garlic
1 1/2 cups sliced cremini mushrooms
1/4 cup pine nuts
2 Tbsp. Bragg Liquid Aminos
1/4 tsp. sea salt
2 handfuls baby spinach

Directions
Heat a large pan over medium-high heat. Add peanut oil and coat surface of pan. Add onion and garlic and fry for about 2 minutes or until fragrant. Add mushrooms and pine nuts; cook for another 2 minutes. Add in cooked rice and mix thoroughly. Add in spinach and Bragg Liquid Aminos and salt. Stir all ingredients together for another minute. Serve warm.

Nutty Quinoa
Serves 4

Ingredients
1 cup quinoa
1/4 cup chopped cashews, toasted
2 Tbsp. fresh lemon juice
2 tsp. extra virgin olive oil
1/4 tsp. Pink Himalayan sea salt
3 green onions, thinly sliced, no white parts

Directions
Prepare quinoa according to package directions. Lightly toast cashews (about 1-2 minutes) in small pan. Add all ingredients to large bowl. Stir well. Serve hot.

NUTRITION PER SERVING | **Fats: 10g • Carbohydrates: 21g • Fiber: 4g
Protein: 4g**

Oven-Roasted Carrots With Feta Cheese
Serves 4

Ingredients
1 1/2 lbs. carrots, peeled and sliced lengthwise into long wedges
1 tsp. grapeseed oil, plus a drizzle for greasing dish
1 Tbsp. red wine vinegar
1 1/2 tsp. honey
dash of Pink Himalayan sea salt
dash of freshly ground black pepper
1 1/2 Tbsp. fresh-squeezed lemon juice
2 oz. feta cheese, crumbled

Directions
Preheat oven to 400 degrees. Lightly wipe casserole dish with grapeseed oil.
Add carrots, 1 tsp. grapeseed oil, vinegar and honey to baking dish. Season
with salt and pepper and mix to evenly coat carrots. Put carrots in oven, mixing occasionally, for about 25 minutes.

Remove from oven, toss with lemon juice and let cool to room temperature.
Add feta, season with additional pepper, toss and serve.

Potato Wedge Fries
Serves 4-6

Ingredients
4 large potatoes
1/4 cup grapeseed oil
1 Tbsp. Parmesan cheese
1 tsp. Pink Himalayan sea salt
1 Tbsp. paprika
dash of pepper
dash of garlic powder

Directions
Heat oven to 350 degrees.
Cut potatoes into wedges and place skin down in a baking dish.
Mix the rest of the ingredients together and brush onto potatoes.
Bake for 1 hour. Remove from oven. Serve hot with ketchup.

NUTRITION PER SERVING | Fats: 3.5g • Carbohydrates: 29g • Fiber: 2g
Protein: 3g

Raisin & Grape Quinoa
Serves 2-4

Ingredients
1 Tbsp. white balsamic vinegar
2 tsp. extra virgin olive oil
1/4 tsp. Pink Himalayan sea salt
15 seedless grapes, halved
1/2 cup raisins
1 cup quinoa, cooked according to package directions

Directions
Add cooked quinoa to large mixing bowl. Add balsamic vinegar, olive oil, salt, grapes and raisins. Mix well and serve.

NUTRITION PER SERVING | **Fats: 8g • Carbohydrates: 16g • Fiber: 4g Protein: 4g**

Raisin & Pine Nut Asparagus
Serves 4

Ingredients
1 lb. asparagus, trimmed
1 Tbsp. grapeseed oil
1/2 small onion, sliced
2 Tbsp. pine nuts
2 1/2 Tbsp. orange juice
3 Tbsp. raisins
2 tsp. honey
1/4 tsp. freshly grated orange rind
dash of Pink Himalayan sea salt

Directions
Boil asparagus for about 3 minutes until tender, yet crisp. Drain and set aside. While asparagus is cooking, heat grapeseed oil in a medium pan and add onion and pine nuts. Cook for about 3 minutes, stirring often. Stir in orange juice, raisins and honey. Cook about 3 minutes, then stir in salt and orange rind. Place asparagus on plate. Spoon orange mixture over asparagus.

Raisin Broccoli
Serves 4

Ingredients
2 tsp. grapeseed oil
6 cups broccoli florets (about 1 head)
1/4 tsp. Pink Himalayan sea salt
1/2 cup raisins
1/4 cup water

Directions
Heat grapeseed oil in a large pan over medium heat. Add broccoli and salt. Mix well. Cook about 3 minutes. Add 1/4 cup water. Cover, put on low heat and cook until broccoli is tender, yet crisp (about 4 minutes). Add in raisins and mix well. Serve and enjoy!

NUTRITION PER SERVING | **Fats: 6g • Carbohydrates: 10g • Fiber: 2g Protein: 3g**

Roasted Cheesy Tomatoes
Serves 4

Ingredients
1 small garlic clove, minced
1 1/2 Tbsp. grapeseed oil
1/2 cup gluten-free panko
4 plum tomatoes, halved
3 tsp. grated Parmigiano-Reggiano cheese
dash of Pink Himalayan sea salt
dash of freshly ground black pepper
1 tsp. grated lemon rind

Directions
Heat broiler to 400 degrees.
Next, mix lemon rind, pepper and garlic together in a small bowl. Mix in panko and grapeseed oil. Place tomato halves on a baking sheet and brush with grapeseed oil. Add a little of the panko mixture to the top of each tomato along with some cheese and salt. Broil 3 minutes or until cheese is bubbly. Serve warm.

Roasted Chickpeas
Serves 2-4

Ingredients
1 can (14 oz.) chickpeas, drained
1 Tbsp. grapeseed oil
1 tsp. cinnamon
1 tsp. nutmeg
2 Tbsp. maple syrup
dash of sea salt

Directions
Preheat oven to 450 degrees.
Spread chickpeas on baking sheet and bake for about 40 minutes.
Put rest of ingredients in large bowl.
When chickpeas are done cooking, transfer them to the bowl and coat with the remaining ingredients.
Enjoy!

NUTRITION
PER SERVING | **Fats: 21g • Carbohydrates: 2g • Fiber: 1g
Protein: 1g**

Roasted Parmesan Broccoli
Serves 2

Ingredients
1 bunch broccoli florets
3 Tbsp. of grapeseed oil
dash of Pink Himalayan sea salt
freshly ground black pepper
Parmesan cheese, freshly grated

Directions
Heat oven to 500 degrees.

Place the broccoli florets onto the aluminum sheet pan and drizzle with grapeseed oil. Add a couple dashes of Pink Himalayan sea salt. Roast for 12-15 minutes.

Remove pan from oven and add a couple dashes of pepper and Parmesan cheese. Serve hot!

Rosemary & Thyme Asparagus
Serves 4

Ingredients
1 sweet onion, chopped
4 oz. crimini mushrooms, sliced
2 Tbsp. grapeseed oil
1 lb. fresh asparagus, thick ends trimmed
2 tsp. fresh rosemary
1 tsp. fresh thyme
1 clove garlic, minced
dash of sea salt
dash of pepper

Directions
Sauté onions, asparagus and garlic in grapeseed oil about 5 minutes.
Add mushrooms, rosemary and thyme, salt and pepper and heat for about 5 more minutes, stirring often.
Cover and cook another 5-8 minutes until asparagus is tender.
Serve and enjoy!

NUTRITION PER SERVING | **Fats: 2.5g • Carbohydrates: 117g • Fiber: 30g Protein: 44g**

Sautéed Mushroom & Garlic String Beans
Serves 5-6

Ingredients
2 lbs. fresh (or frozen) organic green beans
9 large shiitake mushrooms (fresh, not dried)
4-5 medium cloves of garlic, minced

Directions
Wash beans, cut off ends, and snap them in half.
Steam the green beans until tender. Drain and set aside.
Coat large pan with grapeseed oil and place on low-medium heat.
Add garlic and mushrooms and cook for 3 minutes, stirring occasionally.
Mix in the green beans and sauté for 6-8 minutes, until beans are browned.
Serve with quinoa, fish or chicken.

Smokey Tortilla Chips
Serves 2-4

Ingredients
gluten-free tortillas, cut into triangles
1 Tbsp. grapeseed oil
dash of smoked paprika
dash of sea salt

Directions
Preheat oven to 350 degrees.
Place tortilla pieces on baking sheet and brush with grapeseed oil.
Sprinkle with salt and smoked paprika.
Bake about 8 minutes until crisp.
Serve and enjoy!

NUTRITION PER SERVING | **Fats: 14g • Carbohydrates: 12g • Fiber: 4g
Protein: 6g**

Spinach Stuffed Mushrooms
Serves 2-4

Ingredients
8 oz. package of white button mushrooms
3 large cloves of garlic, minced
4 cups of baby spinach leaves, chopped (hard stems removed)
2 Tbsp. nutritional yeast or Parmesan, shredded
sea salt & pepper
2 Tbsp. grapeseed oil

Directions
Preheat oven to 400 degrees.
Wash mushrooms. Remove and mince the stems. Set stems aside.
Heat grapeseed oil in medium pan and add garlic and mushroom stems.
Sauté about 3-5 minutes and add spinach. Cook until wilted. Add salt and pepper, mix well and remove from heat.
Line up mushrooms on baking sheet and stuff them with the spinach mixture.
Sprinkle with nutritional yeast or Parmesan cheese and bake for about 20 minutes.
Serve hot.

NUTRITION
PER SERVING

Fats: 15g • Carbohydrates: 24g • Fiber: 11g
Protein: 3g

Strawberry Avocado Salsa
Serves 2-4

Ingredients
2 cups fresh strawberries, diced
1 jalapeño, finely chopped
1 avocado, diced
1/4 cup red onion, diced
fresh cilantro
splash of lime juice

Directions
Marinate 30 minutes and serve with your favorite organic chips.

NUTRITION
PER SERVING

Fats: 7g • Carbohydrates: 21g • Fiber: 6g
Protein: 8g

Sugar Snap Pea Skillet
Serves 2-4

Ingredients
1 Tbsp. grapeseed oil
8 oz. cremini mushrooms, trimmed and sliced
2 1/2 cups sugar snap peas, trimmed
1 cup scallions, chopped
2 cloves garlic, minced
1 Tbsp. Bragg Liquid Aminos, to taste

Directions
Heat grapeseed oil in a large pan over medium heat. Add mushrooms, snap peas and scallions and cook, stirring continually for about 4 minutes. Add garlic and cook, stirring, until browned, about 1 minute. Stir in Bragg Liquid Aminos and cook for another 5 minutes. Serve and enjoy!

Sweet Potato Fries
Serves 2-3

Ingredients
2 large sweet potatoes
3 Tbsp. agave (or honey)
dash of sea salt
2 Tbsp. grapeseed oil

Directions
Preheat oven to 375 degrees.
Wash and peel potatoes and cut into thin, French-fry-like strips.
In large bowl, combine 1 Tbsp. grapeseed oil and salt.
Toss sweet potatoes in mixture.
Spread 1 Tbsp. grapeseed oil over baking sheet and spread out potatoes in single layer.
Bake about 30 minutes or until tender on the inside and crispy on the outside.
Transfer to serving plate. Add honey to small bowl for dipping.
Enjoy!

NUTRITION
PER SERVING

Fats: 8g • Carbohydrates: 22g • Fiber: 2g
Protein: 25g

Veggie Tray With Dolce Mint Tzatziki Dip
Serves 2-4

Ingredients
Vegetables: Broccoli, small carrots, cherry tomatoes, celery slices or your favorites! (Option: This dip also goes well with pita chips.)

For Dip
2 (8 oz.) containers plain Greek yogurt - or soy yogurt (vegan option)
2 cucumbers, diced small
1 Tbsp. olive oil
1/2 lemon, juiced
sea salt & pepper (to taste)
1 Tbsp. chopped fresh mint leaves
3 cloves garlic, chopped small

Instructions
Wash vegetables, then chop and set aside.

To Make Dip
Combine all ingredients well.
Cover and refrigerate for at least 1 hour.
Serve cold with veggies or pita chips!

FOOD | FACTOIDS

MINT

Nauseous? Mint is a natural anti-nausea remedy. Mint or peppermint teas are great for soothing achy bellies. Mint is also a great palate cleanser. Keep it in mind next time you are eating foods with big flavor differences.

NUTRITION PER SERVING | Fats: 12g • Carbohydrates: 71g • Fibers: 8g
Protein: 13g

Whole Grain Shiitake & Pea Risotto
Serves 4

Ingredients
4 cups organic free-range chicken broth (we like Pacific and Imagine brands)
1 Tbsp. grass-fed butter
1/2 cup onion, finely chopped
1 1/2 tsp. minced garlic
1 cup uncooked short grain brown rice
1/2 cup organic apple juice
1 Tbsp. grapeseed oil
2 handfuls baby spinach
4 cups shiitake mushroom caps, thinly sliced
3/4 cup organic frozen green peas
6 Tbsp. grated fresh Parmesan cheese
1/4 tsp. freshly ground black pepper

Directions
Add broth to a medium pot and bring to a simmer. In a large pan, heat grass-fed butter over medium heat. Next, add onion and 1 tsp. of the garlic, stirring constantly. Next, add the rice; cook 2 minutes, stirring constantly. Add apple juice; cook 2 minutes, stirring until liquid is absorbed. Stir in 1/2 cup broth; cook 2 minutes, stirring until liquid is absorbed.

Continue to add the remaining broth, about a half cup at a time. Allow broth to absorb into mixture before adding more broth. Next, heat oil in a large pan over medium heat. Add mushrooms; sauté 5 minutes or until tender. Add spinach and sauté, stirring often. As spinach wilts, add remaining garlic; stir well and set aside. Finally, stir mushrooms, spinach, peas, 4 Tbsp. cheese and pepper into risotto; cook about 4 minutes.

Serve risotto in bowls and top with a sprinkle of cheese.

Zucchini In Red Sauce
Serves 2-4

Ingredients
2 zucchinis, peeled & sliced
2 Tbsp. grapeseed oil
1 15-oz. can diced tomatoes
dash of sea salt
dash of pepper

Directions
In a small pan, sauté zucchini in grapeseed oil until tender and then add diced tomatoes and gently stir.
Add salt and pepper and serve.

SMOOTHIES

NUTRITION PER SERVING | **Fats: 5g • Carbohydrates: 46g • Fiber: 8g**
Protein: 8g

Apple & Kale Smoothie
Serves 1

Ingredients
1 apple
1 carrot
small handful kale
1 cup water
1/2 cup ice
1 Tbsp. ground flaxseed
1 Tbsp. hemp oil
1 tsp. agave

Directions
Blend together and enjoy!

NUTRITION PER SERVING | **Fats: 50g • Carbohydrates: 64g • Fiber: 23g Protein: 34g**

Banana Almond Butter Smoothie
Serves 1-2

Ingredients
1 banana
1/2 cup strawberries
1/2 cup plain Greek yogurt or almond milk
2 Tbsp. carob nibs
1/4 cup almond butter
1 cup ice
1 Tbsp. ground flaxseed
2 Tbsp. water

Directions
Blend together and enjoy!

NUTRITION PER SERVING	**Fats: 88g • Carbohydrates: 52g • Fiber: 15g** **Protein: 10g**

Berry Coconut Almond Smoothie
Serves 1

Ingredients
1 heaping cup frozen mixed berries (blackberries, raspberries, strawberries, blueberries)
1 1/2 cups coconut milk
1/2 banana (fresh or frozen)
1 tsp. dry chia seeds

Directions
Add all ingredients to blender and blend on high speed until smooth. Serve cold!

Blueberry Banana Almond Smoothie
Serves 1

Ingredients
1 cup frozen organic blueberries
1 Tbsp. almond butter
1/2 banana
1 cup almond milk

Directions
Place all of the ingredients in a blender and blend at high speed until smooth.

NUTRITION
PER SERVING | Fats: 0.5g • Carbohydrates: 58g • Fiber: 7g
Protein: 6g

Blueberry Date Banana Smoothie
Serves 1-2

Ingredients
1 cup blueberries
1 banana
2 dates
1 cup water
1/2 cup ice
1 Tbsp. ground flaxseed
1 Tbsp. hemp oil
1 tsp. agave

Directions
Blend together and enjoy!

The B.O.P. Smoothie (Banana Oatmeal Peanut)
Serves 1-2

Ingredients
2 Tbsp. oat bran
2 to 3 Tbsp. hot or boiling water (enough to just cover the oats)
1 cup unsweetened almond milk
1/2 tsp. organic vanilla
1 frozen banana, sliced
1 Tbsp. peanut butter
1 tsp. agave nectar
1 tsp. dry chia seeds

Directions
Mix oat bran and boiling water in a bowl and let sit until thickened (about 10 minutes). Next, put the oat bran and the rest of the ingredients in a blender and blend at high speed for about 1 minute or until smooth. Serve immediately.

NUTRITION
PER SERVING

Fats: 8g • Carbohydrates: 124g • Fiber: 18g
Protein: 11g

Citrus Smoothie
Serves 1-2

Ingredients
2 oranges
4 clementines
1 cup fresh pineapples
1 banana
1 cup almond milk or 4 oz. plain Greek yogurt
1 cup ice
1 Tbsp. ground flaxseed
1 Tbsp. hemp oil

Directions
Blend together and enjoy!

FOOD | FACTOIDS

BANANA

Bananas can help stave off muscle cramps
during workouts and leg cramps during sleeping
due to their high potassium content,
which helps with muscle contractions.
Potassium is also great to help reduce bloating.

NUTRITION
PER SERVING | **Fats: 1g • Carbohydrates: 44g • Fiber: 9g
Protein: 4g**

Cucumber Basil Juice
Serves 1

Ingredients
1 cup fresh basil leaves
1 cucumber, peeled
1 lime, peeled
1 apple, pitted and cored

Directions
Juice all ingredients together and serve over ice.

Cucumber, Kale & Apple Juice
Serves 1

Ingredients
1 cucumber
1 handful kale
2 stalks celery
1 broccoli stem
1 apple
1/2 lemon, peeled

Directions
Juice all ingredients together and serve over ice.

NUTRITION | Fats: 0.5g • Carbohydrates: 48g • Fiber: 12g
PER SERVING | Protein: 4g

Cucumber Pear Juice
Serves 1

Ingredients
1 cucumber
1 pear
1/4 cup fresh mint
1 lemon, peeled
1 handful baby spinach

Directions
Juice all ingredients together and serve over ice.

Cucumber Water
Makes 128, 8 oz. glasses

Ingredients
1 cucumber, peeled and sliced into wheels
1 gallon water

Directions
Combine water and cucumbers into glass jar and let sit for a few hours so water absorbs the cucumber flavor. Serve cold!

NUTRITION
PER SERVING | **Fats: 2g • Carbohydrates: 29g • Fiber: 5g
Protein: 2g**

Green Strawberry Smoothie
Serves 1

Ingredients
2 cups strawberries
1/4 cup blueberries
1 head of broccoli
1 carrot
1 cup water
1/2 cup ice
1 Tbsp. ground flaxseed
1 Tbsp. hemp oil
1 tsp. agave

Directions
Blend together and enjoy!

**Fats: 15g • Carbohydrates: 50g • Fiber: 17g
Protein: 23g**

Kiwi Mango Smoothie
Serves 1-2

Ingredients
1 cup fresh mango
1 cup fresh kiwi
1/4 cup buckwheat
handful baby spinach
1 cup water
1/2 cup ice
1 Tbsp. ground flaxseed
1 Tbsp. hemp oil
1 tsp. agave

Directions
Blend together and enjoy!

NUTRITION
PER SERVING | **Fats: 5g • Carbohydrates: 46g • Fiber: 4g
Protein: 8g**

Melon, Date & Kale Smoothie
Serves 1

Ingredients
2 cups honeydew melon
handful kale
2 dates
1 cup water
1/2 cup ice
1 Tbsp. ground flaxseed
1 Tbsp. hemp oil
1 tsp. agave

Directions
Blend together and enjoy!

FOOD|FACTOIDS

HEMP SEEDS

Hemp seeds contain all essential amino acids, making them an ideal protein source for vegans and vegetarians! They're also an excellent source of fiber and act as an antioxidant. Since hemp seeds come from the Cannabis plant (yes, the same one that marijuana comes from), it does contain very small traces of THC—however, the amount is similar to the amount of opium found in poppy seeds.

SMOOTHIES

| **Fats: 4.5g • Carbohydrates: 61g • Fiber: 12g Protein: 10g**

Mike's Green Power Drink
Serves 1-2

A great pre and post workout snack!

Ingredients
large handful kale
large handful baby spinach
1 cup broccoli
2 carrots
1 apple
1 cup water (or 1/2 cup almond milk & 1/2 cup water)
1/2 cup ice
1 Tbsp. ground flaxseed
1 Tbsp. hemp oil
1 tsp. agave

Directions
Blend together and enjoy!

NUTRITION
PER SERVING

**Fats: 0.5g • Carbohydrates: 80g • Fiber: 20g
Protein: 4g**

Orange Spinach Juice
Serves 1

Ingredients
1 1/2 cup baby spinach
1 apple
2 lemons, peeled
1 lime, peeled
2 oranges, peeled
1 celery stalk
1/2-inch fresh ginger, finely grated

Directions
Juice all ingredients together and serve over ice.

NUTRITION
PER SERVING

| Fats: 10g • Carbohydrates: 55g • Fiber: 8g
| Protein: 8g

Peach Almond Smoothie
Serves 1

Ingredients
2 Tbsp. oat bran
2 to 3 Tbsp. hot or boiling water (enough to just cover the oat bran)
1 1/2 large ripe peaches, sliced, or 8 oz. frozen peaches
1 cup unsweetened almond milk
10 raw almonds
1 1/2 to 2 tsp. agave nectar (to taste)
couple of ice cubes if using fresh fruit

Directions
Combine oat bran and boiling water in a bowl and let sit, about 10 minutes, until thickened.
Next, put the oat bran and the rest of the ingredients in a blender and blend on a high speed for about 1 minute or until smooth. Serve immediately.

NUTRITION
PER SERVING | Fats: 14g • Carbohydrates: 42g • Fiber: 4g
Protein: 24g

Peanut Butter, Banana, Hemp Seed Smoothie
Serves 1

Ingredients
1/2 cup almond milk
1/2 cup vanilla fat-free yogurt
2 tsp. hemp seeds
1 tsp. chia seeds
1 Tbsp. peanut butter
1 tsp. honey
1/2 ripe banana, sliced
3-4 ice cubes

Directions
Place all of the ingredients in a blender and blend at high speed until smooth.

NUTRITION
PER SERVING

Fats: 5g • Carbohydrates: 49g • Fiber: 4g
Protein: 4g

Rasp-Cherry Ginger Smoothie
Serves 1

Ingredients
1 cup organic frozen raspberries
1/4 cup organic frozen cherries
3/4 cup unsweetened almond milk
1 1/2 Tbsp. honey
2 tsp. grated fresh ginger
1 tsp. hemp seed
1 tsp. chia seed
1 tsp. lemon juice

Directions
Blend all ingredients together on high until smooth. Serve immediately.

NUTRITION
PER SERVING
| Fats: 2g • Carbohydrates: 29g • Fiber: 5g
Protein: 2g

Strawberry Green Tea Smoothie
Serves 1

Ingredients
2 cups green tea, chilled
1 1/2 cups frozen organic strawberries
1/2 cup almond milk
honey

Directions
Add all ingredients into a blender and mix on high until smooth. Serve cold!

**Fats: 11g • Carbohydrates: 93g • Fiber: 19g
Protein: 21g**

Strawberry Spinach Oat Bran Smoothie
Serves 1

Ingredients
1/2 cup oat bran
1 cup frozen strawberries
3/4 cup unsweetened almond milk
1/4 cup plain Greek yogurt
1 Tbsp. chia seeds
1 Tbsp. honey
1 small handful baby spinach

Directions
Add all ingredients to the blender and blend on high process until smooth. Serve cold.

NUTRITION
PER SERVING | **Fats: 5g • Carbohydrates: 70g • Fiber: 11g**
Protein: 19g

Sunrise Orange Smoothie
Serves 1-2

Ingredients
2 oranges peeled
1 banana
1/2 cup strawberries
4 oz. plain Greek yogurt
1 cup ice
1 Tbsp. ground flaxseed
1 Tbsp. hemp oil

Directions
Blend together and enjoy!

NUTRITION PER SERVING | **Fats: 4g • Carbohydrates: 48g • Fiber: 8g Protein: 9g**

Tomato Flax Smoothie
Serves 1-2

Ingredients
2 cups tomatoes
1/2 apple
1 carrot
1 celery stalk
Tabasco or hot sauce, to taste
2 cups ice
1 Tbsp. ground flaxseed
1 Tbsp. hemp oil

Directions
Blend together and enjoy!

DESSERTS & BAKING

NUTRITION PER SERVING | **Fats: 0g • Carbohydrates: 27g • Fiber: 3g Protein: 1g**

Banana Ice Cream
Serves 4

Ingredients
4 frozen bananas
sprinkle of chia seeds

Directions
Using a high-speed blender like a food processor, Vitamix or Blend-tec, blend bananas until smooth and creamy. Scrape out into bowl and freeze for about 20 minutes.
Remove from freezer. Scoop out a serving and top with chia seeds.

**Fats: 0g • Carbohydrates: 26g • Fiber: 4g
Protein: 3g**

Berries & Melon Soup
Serves 4

Ingredients
1 cantaloupe, cut in chunks (will be blended)
6 fresh mint leaves, thinly chopped
1 cup raspberries
1 cup blueberries
1/4 cup Greek yogurt
1 Tbsp. organic orange blossom honey

Directions
Blend cantaloupe in a blender until smooth. Stir in mint. Separate mixture among 4 small bowls. Top each bowl with berries. Mix yogurt and honey together, then add 1 Tbsp. onto each bowl. Serve and enjoy!

DESSERTS & BAKING

NUTRITION PER SERVING | **Fats: 4.5g • Carbohydrates: 13g • Fiber: 1g Protein: 1g**

Cherry & Dark Chocolate Ginger Cookies
Serves 24

Ingredients
3/4 cup whole wheat flour
1/2 tsp. baking soda
1/2 tsp. Pink Himalayan sea salt
1/4 tsp. ground ginger
1 large egg
1/4 cup crystallized ginger, chopped
3/4 cup coconut sugar
1/3 cup grapeseed oil
1 tsp. pure vanilla extract
1/2 cup old-fashioned oats
2 oz. organic dark chocolate chips
1/3 cup dried cherries

Directions
Preheat to 375 degrees.
Whisk flour, baking soda, salt and ground ginger in a small bowl. Whisk egg, coconut sugar, oil and vanilla in a large bowl. Mix the dry and wet ingredients together. Mix in oats, chocolate, cherries and crystallized ginger.

Drop the cookie dough by Tbsp. onto 2 ungreased baking sheets, about 1 1/2 inches apart.
Bake the cookies until golden around the edges, about 10 minutes. Remove from oven and transfer to a cooling rack.

NUTRITION
PER SERVING | **Fat: 1.5g • Carbohydrates: 24g • Fiber: 3g
Protein: 6g**

Cherry Frozen Yogurt
Serves 4

Ingredients
1 (16 oz.) package frozen cherries
2 Tbsp. honey or agave
3/4 cup nonfat Greek yogurt
4 tsp. chia seed

Directions
Add cherries to food processor (Vitamix and Blendtec-type blenders work well here) and pulse until coarsely chopped. Add in yogurt. Process until smooth and creamy. Scoop into serving bowls and drizzle with honey or agave.
Top with a sprinkle of chia seed.

FOOD | FACTOIDS

AGAVE

Agave nectar is naturally low on the glycemic index, scoring a 27, compared to sugar, which scores a 92, making agave a great alternative to sugar for tight blood sugar control.

NUTRITION
PER SERVING

Fat: 1.5g • Carbohydrates: 11g • Fiber: 1g
Protein: 1g

Dark Chocolate Dipped Dates
Serves 20

Ingredients
10 Medjool dates, pitted and soft*
1/2 Tbsp. almond butter
dash of Pink Himalayan sea salt
1/2 cup organic dark chocolate chips
1 tsp. coconut oil
chia seeds
(optional: 20 decorative toothpicks)

*Note: If you are starting with hard dates, soak them for a couple hours in water until soft.

Directions
In a food processor or Vitamix/Blendtec-type blender, process dates with the almond butter until a paste forms. Next, place date mixture in freezer for about 10 minutes. Remove from freezer and, using your hands, shape into 20 balls. Place balls on a cookie sheet. Once finished, put balls in freezer for about 10 minutes.

Next, add chocolate bits with the coconut oil to a small saucepan and melt using a low heat.

Once chocolate melts, remove date balls from freezer and dunk each one into the chocolate. Place on cookie sheet and sprinkle with chia seeds. Stick each ball with a toothpick.

Place balls back into the freezer for 30 minutes. Serve cold.

NUTRITION
PER SERVING | **Fats: 5g • Carbohydrates: 11g • Fiber: 2g**
Protein: 1g

Dark Chocolate Dipped Strawberries
Serves 4

Ingredients
2 oz. organic dark chocolate
15 whole fresh strawberries

Directions
To melt chocolate: Break chocolate into pieces and place in light metal bowl. Set bowl over a pot of lightly steaming water. The steam will slowly cook the chocolate above. Stir until melted.
(You can also put the chocolate in the top of a double boiler if you have one. Place over hot, but not boiling, water. Stir until melted.)
Next, dip strawberries in the melted chocolate and place on parchment paper.

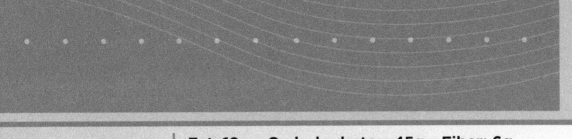

NUTRITION
PER SERVING

Fat: 12g • Carbohydrates: 45g • Fiber: 6g
Protein: 2g

Easy Cinnamon Oat Apples
Serves 2

Ingredients
2 apples
2 Tbsp. grass-fed butter
2 Tbsp. rolled oats
2 Tbsp. coconut sugar
2 Tbsp. 100% white whole wheat flour
dash of cinnamon

Directions
Heat oven to 350 degrees. Hollow out the center of the apples and place each on a square of heavy-duty aluminum foil. Place each of those in a sturdy baking dish. Next, mix the butter, oats, flour, coconut sugar, and cinnamon until lumps form. Place half of the oat mixture into the core of one apple and half of the mixture into the other apple. Wrap the foil around each apple and bake for 30 minutes. Serve warm.

NUTRITION PER SERVING | Fats: 9g • Carbohydrates: 16g • Fiber: 1g
Protein: 2g

Gluten Free Oatmeal Thinnies
Serves 24

Ingredients
1/4 cup rice flour
1 large egg
1 cup grass-fed butter
1 cup coconut sugar
1 Tbsp. pure vanilla extract
1/2 tsp. Pink Himalayan sea salt
2 1/2 cups gluten-free, old-fashioned rolled oats

Directions
Preheat the oven to 350 degrees. Add butter, sugar, vanilla and salt in a medium pot. Melt butter mixture over low heat. Turn off the heat and add the oats and flour to the melted butter mixture and stir well. Add the egg and mix well. Line baking sheets with parchment paper and drop Tbsp. of batter onto baking sheets, leaving 1 1/2 inches of space between each cookie. Flatten each cookie with the back of a spatula. Bake for 12-16 minutes until edges turn light brown. Remove from oven. Allow to cool before removing cookies to cooling rack.

NUTRITION
PER SERVING | **Fats: 12g • Carbohydrates: 12g • Fiber: 1g**
Protein: 4g

Hemp Seed Cashew Butter Cookies
Serves 20

Ingredients
1/2 cup coconut oil (solid)
1/4 cup honey
1/2 cup natural cashew butter
1 egg
1 tsp. pure vanilla extract
1 cup 100% white whole wheat flour
1/4 tsp. salt
1/2 tsp. baking soda
1/2 tsp. baking powder
2 Tbsp. oat bran
1 Tbsp. shelled hemp seeds
1/2 cup peanut butter

Directions
Preheat the oven to 350 degrees.
In a medium mixing bowl, mix the solid coconut oil, honey and cashew butter together with an electric blender until creamy. Add the egg and vanilla and mix well.

In another bowl, combine the flour, salt, baking soda and baking powder. Next, stir in the hemp seed and oat bran.

Combine both mixtures, mix in peanut butter and stir well.

Wipe baking sheets with coconut oil. Using your hands, roll the dough into 1-inch balls and put them on baking sheet about 2 inches apart. Press down on each ball with a fork to create a cross-hatch pattern. Bake for 8-10 minutes. Remove from the oven and allow to cool down for 5 minutes before moving the cookies to a wire rack.

NUTRITION
PER SERVING | **Fats: 5g • Carbohydrates: 19g • Fiber: 1g
Protein: 2g**

Holiday Gingerbread Cookies
Serves 24

Break out your favorite cookie cutters!

Ingredients
2 2/3 cups 100% white whole wheat flour
1 1/2 tsp. baking soda
1/2 tsp. baking powder
1 tsp. cinnamon
1 tsp. ground ginger
1/2 tsp. ground cloves
dash of Pink Himalayan sea salt
1/2 cup molasses
1/2 cup melted coconut oil
1/2 coconut sugar
1/4 cup almond milk
1 tsp. pure vanilla extract

Directions
Preheat oven to 350 degrees. Add dry ingredients to a large bowl and mix well. Whisk together the oil, molasses, coconut sugar, almond milk and vanilla extract.

Mix wet and dry ingredients together. Using your hands or rolling pin, flatten the dough into a large pancake, wrap it in plastic wrap (Saran Wrap), and refrigerate for a minimum of 30 minutes. Add a sprinkle of flour to a clean surface and roll the dough out into a thin layer, about 1/4 inch thick. Using your favorite cookie cutters or shaping tool, cut the dough into desired shapes. Bake cookies on ungreased cookie sheet until edges turn light brown, for 8 minutes. Remove from oven. Wait 2 minutes before transferring to cooling rack.

NUTRITION
PER SERVING

**Fats: 5g • Carbohydrates: 37g • Fiber: 1g
Protein: 3g**

Mango Cups
Serves 2

Ingredients
1 large mango, cut into bite-sized pieces
grated zest and juice of 1 lime
1/2 cup low-fat vanilla yogurt
2 Tbsp. coconut sugar
2 tsp. grass-fed butter

Directions
Heat oven to 400 degrees. Divide mango between 2 small baking tins (or ramekins) and mix in lime zest. Top with 1/4 cup each of yogurt, 1 Tbsp. each of coconut sugar and 1 tsp. each of butter. Drizzle with lime juice. Broil 2 to 3 minutes or just until the topping melts and browns.

Mascarpone Baked Pears
Serves 1-2

Ingredients
1/3 cup mascarpone cheese
1/2 cup apple juice
1 Tbsp. grass-fed butter
dash of cinnamon
2 medium ripe pears
1 tsp. coconut sugar and a dash

Directions
Preheat oven to 375 degrees.

Cut pears in half and core. Place cut side up in baking dish. Pour apple juice into bottom of baking dish. Spoon 1/2 tsp. coconut sugar and a 1/2 tsp. butter into each pear. Bake 30 minutes until pears are tender.

Combine cheese, cinnamon and extra coconut sugar.

Top each pear half with cheese mixture and serve warm.

NUTRITION PER SERVING | **Fats: 12g • Carbohydrates: 28g • Fiber: 2g
Protein: 6g**

No-Bake Honey Brown Rice Bars
Serves 6

Ingredients
3 cups organic brown rice cereal
1/2 cup creamy peanut butter
2 tsp. pure vanilla extract
3-4 Tbsp. honey

Directions
Mix together the peanut butter, vanilla extract and honey until creamy. Stir in the brown rice cereal. Lightly wipe baking sheet with coconut oil. Spread mixture evenly into the pan and press down with a spatula to flatten.

Put in the freezer for an hour. Remove from freezer and cut into small bars. Refrigerate leftovers.

Vanilla Blueberry Yogurt Parfait
Serves 1

Ingredients
1 cup low-fat vanilla yogurt
1/3 cup granola
1/2 cup fresh blueberries, divided

Directions
Spoon about half of the yogurt into the bottom of a glass. Layer half the granola atop the yogurt. Next, add a layer of blueberries. Repeat layering until ingredients are gone. Serve cold.

NUTRITION
PER SERVING

Fats: 5g • Carbohydrates: 30g • Fiber: 3g
Protein: 2g

Wheat-less Banana Strawberry Muffins
Makes 12 big muffins

Ingredients
2 cups light spelt flour
2 bananas
3/4 cup and 2 Tbsp. unsweetened almond milk
1 tsp. apple cider vinegar
1/4 cup pure maple syrup
1 tsp. pure vanilla extract
1/4 cup coconut oil, melted
6 Tbsp. coconut sugar
2 tsp. baking powder
1/2 tsp. baking soda
1 1/2 tsp. cinnamon
1/2 tsp. Pink Himalayan sea salt
1 cup fresh strawberries, chopped (or use whatever fresh berry is in season!)

Directions
Preheat oven to 350 degrees and grease a muffin tin by lightly wiping with coconut oil.

Mash bananas into medium bowl along with the milk, vinegar, maple syrup and vanilla. Do not stir. Melt the coconut oil in a small pot over low heat. Set aside. Next, mix together the dry ingredients in a large bowl. Stir melted coconut oil into the wet mixture. Pour wet ingredients into the dry ingredients and lightly stir. Mix in the strawberries. Do not overmix. Fill each mold in the muffin tin until about 3/4 of the way full. Bake for 25 minutes or until a toothpick comes out clean. Cool in pan for 5 minutes and then transfer muffins to a cooling rack and cool for another 15-20 minutes.

More Resources

TWITTER
Follow Mike Dolce on Twitter @TheDolceDiet and check out his "favorited tweets" for inspirational testimonials!

FACEBOOK
Check out The Dolce Diet fan page at Facebook.com/TheDolceDiet

YOUTUBE
For videos detailing exercises, recipes and so much more, visit The Dolce Diet YouTube channel at YouTube.com/dolcediet

THE DOLCE DIET SOCIAL NETWORK
It's FREE! Design your own profile page at MYDolceDiet.com and talk with Mike during his frequent LIVE CHATS, as well as with others living healthy, vibrant lifestyles just like you!

THE DOLCE DIET OFFICIAL WEBSITE
Get the latest news about Mike, his athletes, health tips and more at TheDolceDiet.com

THE MIKE DOLCE SHOW
Mike answers your questions and chats with featured guests weekly! Listen at TheMikeDolceShow.com, on iTunes or Stitcher, or by downloading our free Android and Apple iOS apps!

THE DOLCE DIET SHOP
Clothing, books, bags and more! Visit DolceDietShop.com today.

#1 BESTSELLING BOOKS BY MIKE DOLCE

The Dolce Diet: LIVING LEAN
The Dolce Diet: 3 WEEKS TO SHREDDED
The Dolce Diet: COLLEGE DIET GUIDE
The Dolce Diet: LIVING LEAN COOKBOOK VOL. 1
The Dolce Diet: HOLIDAY MENU (KINDLE ONLY)
The Dolce Diet: VALENTINE'S DAY MENU (KINDLE ONLY)
Available in paperback & eBook at amazon.com worldwide and in ebook at iTunes (iBooks.)

EXERCISE DVDS BY MIKE DOLCE

UFC FIT - 12-week training program with nutrition and lifestyle manual. Available at UFC-FIT.com

9 780984 963195